Lean for
Service Organizations
and Offices

Also available from ASQ Quality Press:

5S for Service Organizations and Offices: A Lean Look at Improvements
Debashis Sarkar

Managing Service Delivery Processes: Linking Strategy to Operations
Jean Harvey

The Executive Guide to Understanding and Implementing Lean Six Sigma:
The Financial Impact
Robert M. Meisel, Steven J. Babb, Steven F. Marsh, and James P. Schlichting

Transactional Six Sigma for Green Belts: Maximizing Service and Manufacturing Processes
Samuel E. Windsor

Managing the Customer Experience: A Measurement-Based Approach
Morris Wilburn

Applying the Science of Six Sigma to the Art of Sales and Marketing
Michael J. Pestorius

Lean Kaizen: A Simplified Approach to Process Improvements
George Alukal and Anthony Manos

A Lean Guide to Transforming Healthcare: How to Implement Lean Principles in Hospitals,
Medical Offices, Clinics, and Other Healthcare Organizations
Thomas G. Zidel

Root Cause Analysis: Simplified Tools and Techniques, Second Edition
Bjørn Andersen and Tom Fagerhaug

Competing for Customers and Winning with Value: Breakthrough Strategies for
Market Dominance
R. Eric Reidenbach and Reginald W. Goeke

The Certified Manager of Quality/Organizational Excellence Handbook, Third Edition
Russell T. Westcott, editor

Enabling Excellence: The Seven Elements Essential to Achieving Competitive Advantage
Timothy A. Pine

To request a complimentary catalog of ASQ Quality Press publications,
call 800-248-1946, or visit our Web site at http://qualitypress.asq.org.

Lean for
Service Organizations
and Offices

A Holistic Approach for
Achieving Operational Excellence
and Improvements

Debashis Sarkar

ASQ Quality Press
Milwaukee, Wisconsin

American Society for Quality, Quality Press, Milwaukee 53203
© 2008 by ASQ
All rights reserved. Published 2007
Printed in the United States of America
13 12 11 10 09 08 07   5 4 3 2 1

Library of Congress Cataloging-in-Publication Data

Sarkar, Debashis.
    Lean for service organizations and offices : a holistic approach for achieving operational excellence and improvements / Debashis Sarkar.
        p. cm.
    Includes bibliographical references and index.
    ISBN: 978-0-87389-724-2 (soft cover : alk. paper)
    1. Service industries—Management—Handbooks, manuals, etc. 2. Industrial management—Handbooks, manuals, etc. I. Title.

    HD9980.65.S27 2007
    658—dc22   2007034601

ISBN: 978-0-87389-724-2

Publisher: William A. Tony
Acquisitions Editor: Matt T. Meinholz
Project Editor: Paul O'Mara
Production Administrator: Randall Benson

ASQ Mission: The American Society for Quality advances individual, organizational, and community excellence worldwide through learning, quality improvement, and knowledge exchange.

Attention Bookstores, Wholesalers, Schools, and Corporations: ASQ Quality Press books, videotapes, audiotapes, and software are available at quantity discounts with bulk purchases for business, educational, or instructional use. For information, please contact ASQ Quality Press at 800-248-1946, or write to ASQ Quality Press, P.O. Box 3005, Milwaukee, WI 53201-3005.

To place orders or to request a free copy of the ASQ Quality Press Publications Catalog, including ASQ membership information, call 800-248-1946. Visit our Web site at www.asq.org or http://qualitypress.asq.org.

Printed in the United States of America

 Printed on acid-free paper

 Quality Press
600 N. Plankinton Avenue
Milwaukee, Wisconsin 53203
Call toll free 800-248-1946
Fax 414-272-1734
www.asq.org
http://www.asq.org/quality-press
http://standardsgroup.asq.org
E-mail: authors@asq.org

To my daddy who is among the stars
and the almighty whose hands silently steer all my endeavors

Table of Contents

List of Figures, Tables, and Exhibits

Preface

Lean, as a concept, has been around for more than five decades. The work of James Womack and Daniel Jones in the 1990s popularized its adoption among manufacturing companies. With the ushering in of the 21st century, we now see it being leveraged by service companies.

Globally, service companies are realizing that interventions such as lean are a must in order to remain competitive. In the coming years, only companies that are efficient and able to meet the changing needs of customers will be able to survive the fierce competition of the marketplace. And relentless elimination of waste using approaches such as lean will be of immense help. Companies that adopt lean will be in a better position to build an intimate relationship with customers and create a foundation of operational excellence.

Lean as a philosophy is new to service companies, and many of them are struggling to determine the correct approach to its adoption. Many of them are declaring early victory after a few successful projects only to realize that the benefits are not sustained over a period of time. One of the reasons why this is happening is because they do not really know what it takes for a holistic lean implementation in a service organization. Little do they realize that a journey of lean requires implementation of a whole lot of things that need to work in tandem with the teams in the center.

Today, if Toyota is a successful company, it's because of their full adoption of lean principles over the last 50 years and making them a part of their organizational fabric. Lean as a way of doing business has helped Toyota to deliver sustained results over many years. In 2003 Toyota surpassed Ford Motor Company as the world's number two automaker in annual global vehicle sales, and analysts say it is on track to surpass General Motors in the coming years.

Lean methodology has the ability to address a wide range of problems faced by service companies, some of which include complexity reduction, sales force productivity enhancement, operations risk control, cost leadership, combining scale with flexibility, service excellence, and improving employee morale and involvement.

My friends who are CEOs and business leaders in service companies often ask me how they should go about implementing lean in their company. This book is the answer to their queries and questions.

Many of the principles that will be discussed in the book are based on what I have successfully implemented myself. Being written from a practitioner's viewpoint, there is less of theory and more of application.

The approach recommended in this book (called the DEB-LOREX model) is just one of the ways by which service companies can go about adopting the lean philosophy. As a student of quality improvement I am sure that there may be many other successful approaches being developed that will sooner or later come to light. I would appreciate your feedback and comments at authors@asq.org.

Debashis Sarkar

Note to Readers

The term *DEB-LOREX model* stands for *Deb's lean organizational excellence model,* which has been created by the author to facilitate lean transformation in service organizations.

The words "DEB-LOREX model," "DEB-LOREX management system," "lean management system," and "house of lean management system" have been used synonymously.

The acronyms "DLMS" and "LMS" have also been used interchangeably. DLMS stands for *DEB-LOREX lean management system* while LMS stands for *lean management system.*

Wherever the acronym LMS (lean management system) has been used, it means D-LMS (*DEB-LOREX lean management system*). To avoid confusion in the reader's mind the abbreviation LMS has been used instead of D-LMS.

The book is interspersed with sidebars entitled *Did You Know?* and *Lessons to Ponder.* The *Did You Know?* sidebars provide additional information and insights on specific topics. The *Lessons to Ponder* sidebars contain short nuggets of wisdom for the reader to meditate on.

The names "DEB-LOREX Model," "D–LMS," "DEB-LOREX Management System," "House of Lean Management System," "DEB-LOREX Index," "Lean Maven," and "Lean Navigator" are exclusive creations of the author and he may acquire trademark/ service marks on these names in future.

Though targeted for service companies, the universal nature of the DEB-LOREX model is such that it can be applied also to manufacturing organizations.

1
Introduction

LEAN THINKING

Lean thinking as a concept has been generating a lot of interest among manufacturing and service organizations. Though not new, this philosophy has gotten its due recognition only over the last few years. Suddenly a large number of companies are embarking on a journey of lean implementation. Organizations are also making claims of efficiencies and improvements that they have achieved through the various tools and techniques of lean. Business leaders often ask me what lean is and if it can be applied to their organization.

So, what is lean? Probably the best definition comes from the National Institute of Standards and Technology (NIST) in the United States, which defines lean as "a systematic approach to identifying and eliminating waste (non-value-added activities) through continuous improvement by flowing the product only when the customer needs it (called "pull") in pursuit of perfection." The concept is not new and originally emerged from the Toyota Production System that was created by Taiichi Ohno. However, James Womack and Daniel Jones popularized it through their 1996 best-seller *Lean Thinking: Banish Waste and Create Wealth in Your Corporation*. Their work demystified the concept for the masses and enunciated the list of possibilities that follow from it.

Manufacturing companies have been using lean principles since at least the 1980s. We have learned of the successes in manufacturing companies through the works of Womack, Jones, Anand Sharma, Patricia Moody, Rajan Suri, and Michael George. These individuals have reported success stories from companies such as Maytag Corporation, Trek Bicycle Corporation, Dell Computer, Ingersoll Cutting Tool Company, Beloit Corporation, John Deere, Pella Corporation, and Lantech. India too has seen a few manufacturing companies practicing lean for business excellence, such as TVS Motors, Sundaram Fastener, Sundaram Brake Linings, and Sundaram Clayton. They may not be calling their improvement journey a lean transformation, but if you analyze their efforts closely, they have been instilling all the principles that make lean thinking the DNA of the organization.

LEAN BEYOND MANUFACTURING

Implementation of lean is no longer confined to manufacturing organizations. Today lean is being successfully applied within service companies. However, there are still a large number of service companies who are looking for a recipe to apply lean to their business processes. A large number of companies are applying lean, but it is confined to only a few processes without many breakthrough results.

What is required today is a holistic approach that can help service companies to gather benefits from the implementation of the lean philosophy. Just applying a few tools and techniques on a few service processes could deliver some benefit, but one can not extract the full value of lean with this approach. Such an ad hoc approach will not impact the overall performance of the organization. Successful implementation of lean requires that it be adopted as a business strategy that has a sustained positive impact on business objectives. The reason lean has been successful in companies such as Toyota is because it has become a way of doing business. So if service companies want to leverage the real power of lean, it should be implemented in a holistic manner. This book provides you with an approach that, if adopted, can give you sustained value over a period of time.

LEAN AND SERVICE ECONOMIES

Lean as an approach is extremely relevant to all countries whose economies are dependent on services. Going forward, only those companies that provide cost advantage and customer convenience will survive in the marketplace. And lean can provide an antidote to both these concerns, as it not only improves organizational efficiency but also improves customer convenience and business profitability. The potential for lean application can be gauged from the percentage of the service sector in the GDP figures of major economies of the world as shown in Table 1.1. "Service" comprises sectors such as government, banking, tourism, retail, education, restaurants, consulting, media, entertainment, heathcare, hospitals, hospitality, and so on. As is obvious from Table 1.1, other than China, in all other countries the service sector comprises more than 50 percent of GDP.

ADDRESSING SYMPTOMS HAS LIMITED VALUE

With the objective of staying profitable, service companies have traditionally taken up cost-cutting programs to reduce operating expenditures. For example, companies focus on cutting down on employee travel, business off-sites, and hotel stays with the hope that it will bring cost efficiency. While the intentions are admirable, this approach is not correct. If the concern is that employee travel costs are high in a company, don't just put an embargo on travel. The approach should be to find out the reasons why employees are traveling more and what steps could be taken to arrest the causes. Unfortunately, fixing symptoms is the norm in many companies. While this works for a time it can not deliver true operational excellence, which these companies are really striving for.

Table 1.1   Percentage of service sector in major economies of the world (as of 2005).

Number	Country	Percentage of Service Sector in GDP
1	United States	78.7
2	Japan	72.5
3	Germany	69.5
4	China	40
5	United Kingdom	75.8
6	France	76.4
7	Italy	68.8
8	Spain	66.5
9	Canada	68.4
10	Brazil	51
11	South Korea	52
12	India	54
13	Mexico	70
14	Russia	57
15	Australia	75

Source: www.cia.gov/cia/publications/factbook.
The order of listing of the countries does not necessarily indicate the rank of the economies.

RELEVANCE OF LEAN TO SERVICE COMPANIES

Despite technology and training interventions, customers are faced with long lead times and unpredictable error rates. A management system built around lean is not only an enabler of achieving operational excellence but also helps to bring flexibility in the way operations are managed. What service companies require in the future is to develop robust, waste-free, flexible processes, while also keeping the views of the customer paramount as the processes are executed. Only those companies that have an efficient business operation and are uniquely able to meet customer needs will be in a position to survive in the marketplace.

This need for lean is further echoed by various research studies carried out across industries.

Banking

IBM Consulting Service's article "The Paradox of Banking 2015: Achieving More By Doing Less" states:

> The future will require superior efficiency and operational excellence from all banks, while industry leadership will be attained by those institutions most adept at harnessing product, service, and process innovation to anticipate and meet customer needs. Ultimately, banks will have to focus on their core strengths—

those activities in which they excel—and partner with best-in-class specialists for everything else: achieving more by doing less (Hedley et al. 2005).

Aviation

Electronic Data Systems' white paper *Agile Airline Enterprise* asserts that:

> Today's airline industry is undergoing more transformation than ever before. The combination of ongoing global economic events, "wired" passengers, and growth of low-cost carriers makes this market ever more competitive on price, cost, and yield. As you assess new and emerging trends such as business process outsourcing and utility computing, you should also explore how your airline's information environment can be designed to make your enterprise more responsive, more flexible and, above all, more agile (Abe et al. 2005).

Giovanni Bisignani, Director General of the International Air Transport Association (IATA), quoted in an article on airsider.net in 2005 on the global outlook for the airline industry, stated:

> Our customers demand that we evolve to a low-cost industry with simplified business processes. Our partners, including air navigation service providers (ANSPs) and airports, must be a part of that evolution. As customers paying an enormous bill, we demand better value, increased transparency, and meaningful consultation on future developments. ANSPs must harmonize infrastructure and operations across borders. And we must agree on the adoption of new technology based on real value and business benefits (Bisignani 2005).

The number of low-cost airlines are also proliferating in the sky. Survival of many of these airlines will require application of lean principles, which help to not only drive down cost but also bring about overall efficiency improvement and service excellence.

Healthcare

Today, healthcare services are burdened with a lot of wasteful practices. To quote Microsoft's white paper *Future of Information Work: Healthcare 2015:*

> Today's challenges are primarily around closing the technology gap in the healthcare industry and eliminating the wasteful practices that claim 50 cents of every healthcare dollar spent in the U.S. economy. In 10 years, it is likely that many of today's systemic inefficiencies will be addressed, and the focus will shift toward optimizing practices that are already relatively IT-centric with a goal of making them at once more pervasive and less intrusive, more secure, and more transparent, and more available globally (Rasmus et al. 2005).

A report by Pricewaterhouse Coopers (PwC) titled *2020 HealthCast—Creating a Sustainable Future,* makes a tacit case for lean implementation in healthcare. Compiled from interviews conducted with 580 executives of hospitals and hospital systems, physician groups, payers, governments, medical supply companies, and employers from around the world in 27 countries, the report says:

> By 2020, health spending is projected to account for 21 percent of gross domestic product (GDP) in the US and a median of 16 percent of GDP in other Organization for Economic Cooperation and Development (OECD) countries. In the future, the health spending growth rates of OECD countries are expected to narrow, although the US spending will remain significantly higher than the rest. By 2020, the US, which accounted for 55 percent of OECD health spending in 2003, will account for 50 percent—still a significant sum.

Further, the report says that:

> Sustainable health systems demonstrate some or all of the following seven features:
>
> *Quest for common ground:* A vision and strategy is needed to balance public versus private interests in building an infrastructure and in providing basic health benefits within the context of societal priorities.
>
> A *digital backbone:* Better use of technology and interoperable electronic networks accelerate integration, standardisation, and knowledge transfer of administrative and clinical information.
>
> *Incentive realignment:* Incentive systems ensure and manage access to care while supporting accountability and responsibility for healthcare decisions.
>
> *Quality and safety standardisation:* Defined and enforced clinical standards establish mechanisms for accountability and enhanced transparency, thereby building consumer trust.
>
> *Strategic resource deployment:* Resource allocation appropriately satisfies competing demands on systems to control costs while providing sufficient access to care for the most people.
>
> *Climate of innovation:* Innovation, technology, and process changes are a means to continuously improve treatment, efficiency, and outcomes.
>
> *Adaptable delivery roles and structures:* Flexible care settings and expanded clinical roles provide avenues for care that are centered on the needs of the patient (Henry et al. 2005).

Clear holistic implementation of lean will have a huge role in achieving many of the above features, especially efficiency improvement, quality and safety starndardization, strategic resource deployment, climate of innovation, and adaptable delivery roles and structures.

Technology, Media, and Telecommunication

The Deloitte 2005 research paper *The Trillion Dollar Challenge: Principles for Profitable Convergence* elucidates the future critical success factors for the convergence of the technology, media, and telecommunication industries. Given the potential of this market, one can clearly see the need and relevance of lean principles. To quote from the paper:

Over the next few years, convergence is predicted to have a massive financial impact on technology, media, and telecommunication (TMT) industries. Between 2005 and the end of decade, based on industry analysts' outlooks, the TMT practices of Deloitte members' firms forecast the generation of at least a trillion dollars revenue from emerging convergence products and services.

The research paper also talks about the seven principles of profitable convergence, which are:

1. Convergence must be driven by customer needs, not technology.

2. Commercial creativity will maximize convergence's impact. TMT companies must also invest in understanding how convergence can improve on the legacy business model.

3. Convergence requires mutual benefit for the parties involved.

4. Convergence and divergence can coexist.

5. Laggards lose. Successful convergence challenges and reshapes traditional boundaries.

6. Timing is everything. A convergent product or service needs to be launched at the right time.

7. Convergence winners and losers are ever changing (Brightman 2005).

IT-Enabled Service Outsourcing

By the year 2008, the IT-enabled industry in India is expected to employ over 1.1 million Indians according to studies conducted by NASSCOM and the leading business intelligence company, McKinsey & Co. Market research shows that in terms of job creation, the information technology–enabled services/business process outsourcing (ITES-BPO) industry is growing at over 50 percent per annum. Further, as echoed in a white paper by ValueFirst Messaging Private Ltd., the three main business drivers for the BPO companies are: (1) cost efficiency, (2) process efficiency, (3) employee satisfaction (Bhandari 2004).

On why countries outsource to India, Thomas & Alex Financial Services mentions that the most important reason is "cost benefits." It also states that the value proposition India offers is that you get high-quality expertise at low cost (wwwthomasandalex.com).

A recent white paper by Right Now Technologies and Peppers & Rogers Group states:

> The mission now is to serve better, faster, cheaper—and to make more money in the process. Senior managers expect customer service to improve service quality and lift the top line without cost spikes or losses in efficiency. But the reality is that many customer service organizations have yet to tame the two-headed monster of achieving cost efficiency *and* higher revenue. A number of obstacles, from siloed solutions and clunky processes to misaligned metrics and incentives, still stand in the way (Right Now Technologies and Peppers & Rogers Group 2005).

The success of companies in many of the above sectors will depend on how effectively they are able to provide a superior customer experience while bringing about cost efficiency and revenue enhancement. This means providing customers rapidly with what they want, when they want it, every time. What these companies require is the ability to achieve consistent service excellence backed up by efficient processes that are improved on an ongoing basis. They need to create satisfied customers who become advocates and recommend the company to friends and family.

All this doesn't require technological breakthroughs. It can be achieved by focusing on the basics and utilizing the potential of its teams. As organizations struggle to stay competitive in the marketplace, lean provides a pathway to achieving sustained growth.

LEAN AND OPERATIONAL EXCELLENCE

To the author, lean thinking is an enterprisewide initiative to bring operational excellence to service businesses. It is an approach that facilitates improvement of process efficiency and quality while also delivering quicker service and cost savings.

However, this is possible only when organizations adopt a holistic approach to deployment. One of the approaches to achieve this is the DEB-LOREX model of lean transformation created by the author. This is an approach to managing the organization in a fashion that breeds overall efficiency improvement. This approach to achieving operational excellence is summarized in Figure 1.1.

DEB-LOREX is an acronym for *Deb's lean organizational excellence model.* The word Deb is from the author's first name, Debashis. The words and abbreviations DEB-LOREX model and DEB-LOREX management system, D-LMS, and LMS (lean management system) have been used synonymously and all mean the same thing.

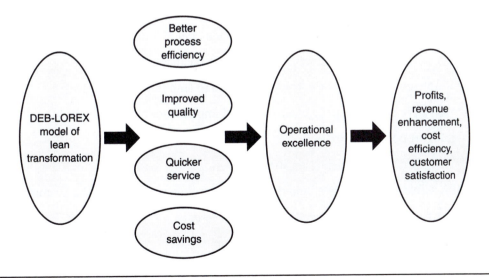

Figure 1.1   DEB-LOREX model of lean transformation and operational excellence.

**ARE YOU WONDERING WHAT THE WORD
DEB-LOREX STANDS FOR?**

It is an acronym for *Deb's lean organizational excellence model.* The word Deb is from the author's first name Debashis. The words and abbreviations DEB-LOREX Model, DEB-LOREX Management System, D-LMS, and LMS (Lean Management System) have been used synonymously and all mean the same thing.

THE DEB-LOREX MODEL

The DEB-LOREX model is a management system for achieving organizational excellence using the principles of lean. Created by the author, it is a transformational time-based approach to achieving sustained benefits through improved service time, lowered costs, and better quality. It is a change management program that endeavors to change the way a company is managed by looking at total ownership of processes and value streams.

It is an enterprisewide movement targeted toward eliminating waste in business systems, processes, and workplaces. The DEB-LOREX model helps to change the mind-set of employees and works toward building capabilities and cultures that support continual improvement, problem prevention, and workplace excellence.

An organization applying the DEB-LOREX model looks at all organizational processes closely from an end-to-end perspective and builds all the capabilities for execution and enablers for ongoing sustainability. It leads to managing the company through processes that cut across functional silos. An underlying belief that drives DEB-LOREX implementation is customer-centricity and declaring war on all activities for which the customer will not pay.

A company implementing the DEB-LOREX model manifests the following traits:

- Adoption of a lean management system as a business strategy

- Visible commitment of the leadership team to lean transformation

- Well-defined vision and a clearly defined implementation plan

- Built around value streams

- Well-defined implementation structure

- Proactive effort to understand the unique and changing needs of the customer

- Business outcomes managed through processes

- End-to-end processes with clear ownership

- Processes in business units segregated into value-creating, value-enabling, and support processes

- High level of process awareness and lean consciousness among employees
- High engagement of employees in the lean implementation
- Metrics of lean management system tied to performance appraisal
- Equitable focus on leading and lagging measures of process performance
- Hierarchy of dashboards as an enabler for business performance
- Focus on both large improvement projects and small improvement projects
- Great emphasis on building capabilities for sustaining LMS
- A focus by leaders on improving processes through measurement
- Regular measurement of process efficiency for all value-creating processes
- Involvement of front-liners and shop-floor colleagues in improvements
- Effort to differentiate the organization through services and new service innovations
- Endeavor to build a problem-prevention mind-set
- Vendors and outsourced agencies are thought of as part of the extended enterprise

Using a model such as DEB-LOREX in lean transformation helps to realign organizational efforts and resources with defined future-state goals of the organization. It leads to the creation of a DNA of ongoing change comprising incremental and breakthrough improvements, with an objective of meeting the changing needs of customers and the marketplace. Though the model has been designed for service companies, manufacturing organizations can also use it. This approach to lean transformation is also called the *house of lean management system* (see Figure 1.2).

THE PHILOSOPHIES THAT DRIVE THE DEB-LOREX MODEL FOR LEAN TRANSFORMATION

It is just not one philosophy that drives the DEB-LOREX model. It has been developed as the confluence of two important philosophies. The foundational philosophy is *lean thinking*, while the thought process that holds it together is *systems thinking*. (See Figure 1.3).

Let us explore each of them to understand their relevance to lean transformation.

Lean Thinking

This is a management approach proposed by Womack and Jones in 1996. As mentioned in *Lean Lexicon: A Graphical Glossary for Lean Thinkers*, the five principles of lean transformation are:

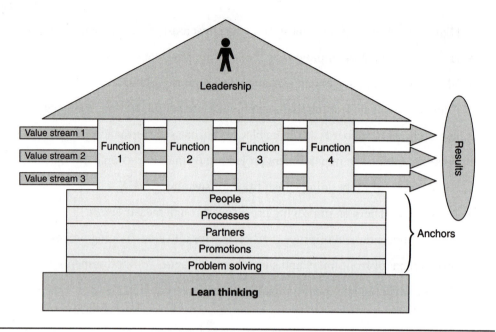

Figure 1.2   The house of lean management system or DEB-LOREX model for lean transformation.

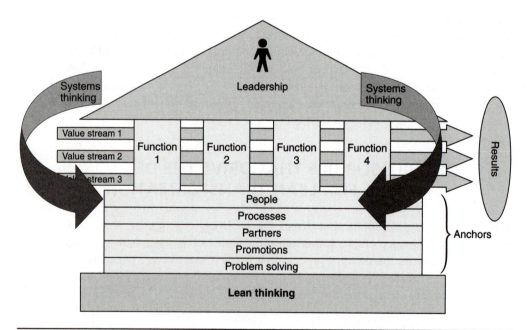

Figure 1.3   The two philosophies that comprise the DEB-LOREX model for lean transformation.

1. Specify value from the standpoint of the end customer by product family

2. Identify all the steps in the value stream for each product family, eliminating whenever possible those steps that do not create value

3. Make the value-creating steps occur in tight sequence so that the product will flow smoothly forward to the next downstream activity

4. As flow is introduced, let customers pull value from the previous upstream activity

5. As value is specified, values streams are identified, wasted steps are removed, and flow and pull are introduced, begin the process again and continue it until a state of perfection is reached in which perfect value is created with no waste

Systems Thinking

This is a philosophy that that helps us understand how things work. It endeavors to go beyond events and reveal the interrelationship of components that are responsible for the pattern of behavior of an event. It is about looking at the world based on these interactions. Systems thinking helps us to look at events and patterns in a different manner. For an organization, having a few excellent departments is not sufficient; what is required is that all departments function well and integrate to achieve the larger objectives of the company.

Systems thinking helps us to look at problems from a different perspective. When a problem occurs, systems thinking goes beyond just correcting the problem to look at methods to arrest and prevent its occurrence. The systems thinker diagnoses problems not just by looking at components of the organization but by looking at how those components interact with each other. Rather than reacting to events, sytems-focused leaders need to look at the practices, processes, and infrastructure that impact the behaviors that determine events.

The relevance of the systems approach to improvement is echoed by Feigenbaum in an article published in *Quality Progress* in 1997:

> Quality has moved from the past focus on management of quality to emphasis on the quality of managing, operating, and integrating the marketing, technology, production, information, and finance areas throughout a company's quality value chain with subsequent favorable impact on manufacturing and service effectiveness (Feigenbaum 1997).

Implementing lean as a system helps us to understand causes and how they impact results. This is what is missing in the lean applications that are happening in service companies.

When the DEB-LOREX model is used as a base for lean transformation, the philosophy of systems thinking has the following effects:

1. Helps to ascertain the cause-and-effect relationships in the overall performance achieved through the application of lean principles

2. Helps to identify the subsystems (value streams and core processes) in the LMS and how they interact with each other

3. Focusing on the interrelationship among the subsystems such as functions, value streams, infrastructure, and so on, ensures that resolving problems in one area does not negatively impact another area of the company

Did You Know?

What is a system?

A *system* is a set of components working toward the achievement of a larger whole. These components are interdependent on each other and interact to contribute toward the unified whole. The system is larger than the sum of its parts. Systems have inputs, processes, outputs, and outcomes. Removing one component from a system will change its basic characteristics. A system is a product of the interactions of the components. In a system what is critical is not only that the individual components are performing well but how all of the components fit together as a whole.

Examples of systems are all around us. They could be either living in nature or could be nonliving. Living systems are cells, organs, and human beings. Nonliving systems are all around us, examples being a car, business organization, management system, and so on.

The following are some of the traits of a system:

1. Every system has a purpose

2. Every system exists within a larger system

3. The properties of a system emerge because of the interaction of the components

4. A system is greater than the sum of its parts

5. Due to interdependence, change in one part of the system will result in change in other parts of the system

6. Systems are goal-oriented and engage in feedback with the environment to meet their goals

7. For survival, a system has to maintain balance and regulation with the supra-system

4. Helps to see the unintended consequences of actions and implementations

5. Helps to identify root causes of problems

The components that make up the DEB-LOREX management system (Figure 1.4) are as follows:

- Leadership

- Functions

- Value streams

- Anchors

- Lean thinking

- Results

For lean to deliver sustained benefits, it is imperative that all the components of the lean management system function in harmony to deliver the desired results. During lean transformation, it is imperative that each of the elements of the DEB-LOREX management system are properly implemented. Inadequacies in any of them will impair the overall expected performance of the organization. The elements comprising leadership, functions, value streams, lean thinking, and anchors are the enablers in the DEB-LOREX model (Figure 1.4). The adequacy of each of the enablers will have direct impact on the

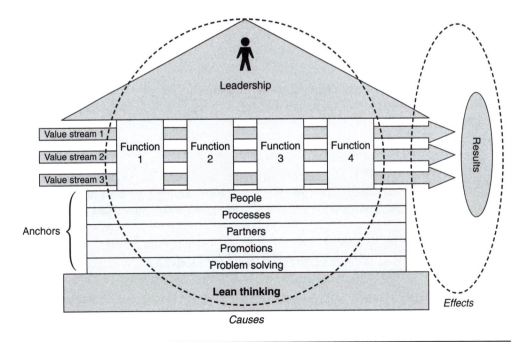

Figure 1.4 Cause-and-effect relationships of the DEB-LOREX model of lean transformation.

Efficiency

The efficiency of a process is defined as its ability to operate within given resources. Resources could be manpower, material, monies, machines, or milieu. Typical efficiency measures include things such as: manpower productivity, cost per unit, process efficiency, and costs of staff and manpower.

Effectiveness

The effectiveness of a process is defined as its ability to meet the requirements of the customer. The customer could be the next person in the process or the end consumer or even stakeholders of an organization. Typical effectiveness measures include things such as market share, customer satisfaction, revenue, and time to market.

performance of the others. For example, an organization may have great processes, but without leadership commitment can not expect the management system to deliver value. As the implementation of lean matures in the company, leaders will be in a position to clearly say which of the enablers (or causes) need to be acted on to achieve the desired results.

Lean Thinking in Detail

Lean thinking is a philosophy that emanated from Toyota. The pioneering work done by Taiichi Ohno at Toyota Motor Company has left a living legacy for all of us to emulate. The subsequent research work done by Womack et al. has provided a brilliant approach to producing operational excellence in organizations, creating value, and meeting organizational objectives by eliminating waste in all forms.

What is waste? *Waste* is any activity or step in a process for which the customer is not willing to pay. Such steps not only add to the time but also the cost of the process. Remember, the words *steps* and *activities* are used interchangeably in this chapter.

WASTES ARE SYMPTOMS

Wastes are actually symptoms of problems in a process. The belief that wastes are the problem is not true. They are manifestations that need to be identified and problem-solved by a structured intervention. All that we do during lean problem solving is to identify waste and understand its causes through the use of lean tools and techniques.

What are symptoms?

Symptoms are signals or indications of problems in a process. Symptoms act as lead indicators or precursors to potential or existing problems in processes or workplaces. They may manifest as abnormalities, complaints, hidden factories, sudden increases in operating expenses, and so on. Mastering the art of identifying symptoms is key to building a continual improvement culture.

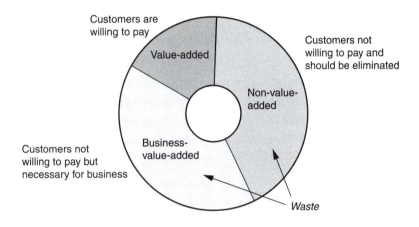

Figure 1.5 Types of waste.

Types of Activities in a Process

There are broadly three types of activities in a process (Figure 1.5):

1. *Value-added steps/activities* are those activities for which the customer is willing to pay. These steps help to bring about a transformation in the product or service being provided by the organization and add a feature or trait that the customer values and is willing to pay for.

   To qualify as value-added, an activity in a process should meet all of the following criteria:

   • It should change the form, feature, feeling, or function that the customer desires

   • It should be done correctly the first time

   • The customer must be willing to pay for it

In the above criteria, the word "feeling" is mentioned because it is of great importance in service companies wherein there could be activities done to improve the customer experience.

2. *Business-value-added steps/activities* are those activities in a process for which the customer is not willing to pay but that can not be avoided. They necessarily need to be present in the process and can not be eliminated from the process. They are also called *necessary non-value-add*. Typically these are activities done for regulators, organizational policies, and so on. The Japanese call them type I *muda* (waste). It is important to note that sometimes to avoid their elimination, over a period of time non-value-added activities get branded as business-value-added steps.

3. *Non-value-added steps/activities* are those activities in a process for which the customers are not willing to pay and can be avoided. The focus should be to eliminate these activities and steps. The Japanese call them type II muda.

It is important to remember that both non-value-added steps and business-value-added steps are actually wastes. When doing waste identification, the tendency is often to brand some of the non-value-added steps as business-value-added steps. This should be avoided at all cost. While doing a lean walk, which we shall discuss later, be critical and look at process steps closely or else you will not get the desired benefits.

So how should each of these steps be treated during a lean intervention? Table 1.2 summarizes for you.

THE EIGHT WASTES OF LEAN

The following are the eight wastes of lean, which have been taken from the work done by Taiichi Ohno. Irrespective of whether you're in a service company or a manufacturing organization, the eight wastes of lean are universally applicable. The examples that have been listed have often been encountered by the author during lean interventions in service processes.

1. *Waste of overproduction.* This is processing more or sooner than required. Examples:

   • Purchasing items before they are needed

Table 1.2   Treatment of process steps under lean.

Types of activities	Type of treatment under lean
Value-added steps	Question and improve
Business-value-added steps	Question and improve
Non-value-added steps	Eliminate

- Processing paperwork before the next person is ready for it

- Franked loan agreements lying unutilized

- More promotional materials printed than required

- Photocopies of forms used instead of printed booklets

2. *Waste of motion.* This is movement of individuals that is unnecessary for successfully completing a job in a process. Examples:

   - Customer services executive having to walk to get brochures and forms in a retail financial services branch

   - Collection agency going to wrong address

   - Multiple visits by salespeople to get the right documents from customers

   - Scattered departments in an organization

   - Walking to/from copier, central filing, fax machine while executing a process

3. *Waste of inventory.* This is when there are items or supplies in the process in excess of what is required for single-piece flow. In a service setting this would mean more supplies or items than required as single-piece flow is often not possible. Examples:

   - Filled in-boxes (electronic and paper)

   - Excessive sales literature/brochures in retail bank branch

   - Piles of loan files lying in branches/offices

   - More stationery than required

   - More IT equipment than required in a workplace

   - Documents/records held beyond retention period

4. *Waste of transportation.* This refers to movement of materials, which is more than just time in processing. Please note that waste of transportation pertains to movement of materials and not people. Examples:

   - Excessive e-mail attachments

   - Multiple hand-offs

   - Multiple approvals

   - Files moving from one branch to another

   - Movement of documents from hub to spoke

   - Multiple movements of cash

   - Couriering/express mail

5. *Waste of waiting.* This refers to individuals and items being idle between operations. This waste is quite evident in setups wherein the loads of process associates are not balanced. Examples:

- Customers waiting in line at a bank branch or ATM
- Files and documents waiting for signatures or approval
- Associates in a process waiting for earlier process to finish
- New employees awaiting infrastructure/computer
- Customer waiting in phone banking/call center queue
- Information technology system downtimes
- Time taken to respond to customer queries

6. *Waste of underutilized people.* This refers to the abilities of associates/employees in a process not being utilized to the fullest. Very often we undermine the creative. Examples:

- Process associates being treated as robots by managers
- Not involving the associates in process improvements
- Not leveraging the qualities of individuals to the fullest
- Not using the creative brainpower of employees
- Not giving the right assignment/work
- Uneven work distribution/load balancing

7. *Waste of defects.* This refers to waste that occurs due to errors and not getting an item or product right the first time out in a process. Due to the errors, the item or the product needs to be reworked. Examples:

- Errors made while filling out the application form of a mortgage customer
- Incorrect name printed on a credit card
- Incorrect data entry
- High rejection rates in savings account opening forms

8. *Waste of overprocessing.* This refers to efforts that add no value for the customer. Examples:

- Redundant steps in a process
- Multiple inspections in a process
- Lack of operator training

- Undefined or unclear customer requirements

- Overdesigning a product or service for a customer

- New products are launched without adequate back-end processes

- Inept design

- Inadequate technology

THE DIMENSION OF TIME IN LEAN

When we talk about a lean intervention in a process, much of the effort is focused on removing time from processes. This is the reason lean thinking is often called *time-based management*.

The following are the various times used in lean in service processes:

- *Cycle time.* This is the time taken to execute an activity in a process. This helps to measure the time taken to complete the smallest unit of work in a process.

- *Value-added time.* This is the time spent in doing value-added activities in a process.

- *Business-value-added time.* This is the time spent on business-value-added steps in a process.

- *Non-value-added time.* This is the time spent on non-value-added steps in a process.

- *Wait time.* This is the time an activity in a process waits to be worked on. It would also include individuals waiting for work in a process. This will be included as a part of non-value-added time.

- *Transport time.* This is the time spent in movement of material or information in a process. The transport time is also called *travel time.*

- *Throughput time.* This is the time taken in the execution of a process. It is the time taken to complete a process from start to finish. Often throughput time gets labeled as *lead time,* which may not be correct. In the manufacturing plant this is often called *door-to-door time.*

- *Lead time.* This is the end-to-end time required for execution of a process, which starts at the time the customer places the order and ends when the customer receives the product or service. The equation for lead time can be expressed as

$$\text{Lead time} = \text{Value-added time} + \text{Business-value-added time}$$
$$+ \text{Non-value-added time}$$

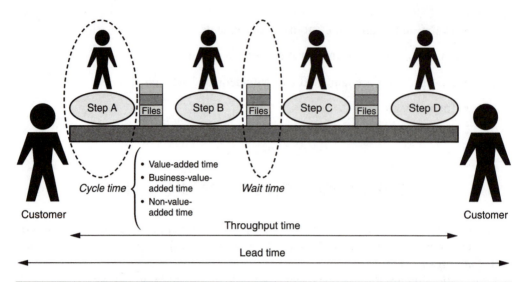

Figure 1.6   Times used in lean.

Looking at Figure 1.6, the equation for lead time can be modified as follows:

$$\text{Lead time} = \text{Cycle time} + \text{Wait time} + \text{Transport time} + \text{Other non-value-added time}$$

Please note that lead time also includes the time taken to deliver the product or service to the customer.

Process Efficiency

Probably one of the most holistic metrics used to ascertain the impact of lean on service processes is *process efficiency*. Process efficiency (also called *value-added-ratio*) is the measurement used to ascertain the non-value-added component in a process. Process efficiency is measured with respect to time and is calculated as per the equation shown below. Typically, the process efficiency of processes should be calculated before and after lean implementation.

$$\text{Process efficiency} = \frac{\text{Value-added time} \times 100}{\text{Total lead time}}$$

As-Is and To-Be State

Facilitating lean in organizations is about taking them from an as-is state to a future state. The application of lean to service companies is shown in Figure 1.7.

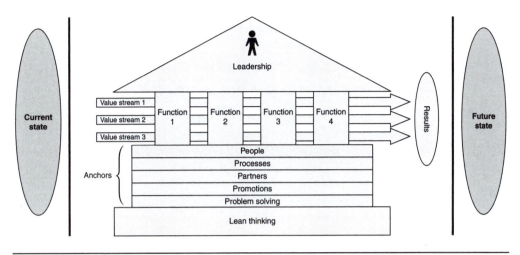

Figure 1.7   Current and future states of lean journey.

Remember, this is a continuous journey. Clearly establish performance metrics on quality, delivery, cost, service, market penetration, capabilities, operating expenses, and so on. Together with future state, you may also want to establish the aspirational state of the organization and the corresponding performance metrics for the same.

THE DEB-LOREX INDEX

The DEB-LOREX index is a holistic measure to ascertain how far an organization is on a journey of lean transformation. The DEB-LOREX index is established by evaluating an organization on a set of parameters based on elements such as leadership, value streams, anchors, customers, and results.

It is recommended that an organization be assessed on a regular basis to ascertain progress. The recommended gap between two assessments should be around three to four months. The gaps found in the assessment serve as inputs for improvements and areas the organization needs to work on.

The process of carrying out the DEB-LOREX management system assessment is detailed in Appendix A.

The DEB-LOREX assessment gives a list of specific action points that need to be worked on to achieve the desired results in a lean transformation.

The Lean Opportunity Checklist

There are times when individuals tell me that their organization is very efficient and do not need the interventions of lean. My response to them is to fill out the Lean Opportunity Checklist (Exhibit 1.1). A positive answer to any of the points indicates that lean has applicability in the company. Go ahead and try out this questionnaire for yourself and see if lean is applicable in your organization.

LESSONS FROM LEAN APPLICATIONS IN THE SERVICE SECTOR

The application of lean in service processes has taught the author a number of lessons that are worth mentioning here. Many of them are generic principles on which the philosophy of lean thinking is based. It is important that we keep this in mind as we commence using lean tools and techniques in process transformation. This will help us understand what drives lean thinking in an organization.

Creativity Before Capital

While improving a process, do not go ahead and just make investments in capital expenditures. First use the capabilities of your team to come up with creative low-cost solutions to remove waste in the processes. Once this is accomplished, you may realize that a capital investment is not required. However, if it is still felt that a capital investment is required, the company should go ahead and do it. More often than not, teams come up with solutions where major expenditures are not required.

Quick and Functional Versus Impeccable Solutions

While implementing lean solutions, do not wait for the impeccable and best solutions. The endeavor should be to get quick results even if they are not the best. Sometimes waiting for the so-called impeccable solution is illusory. It not only takes a lot of time and money, but may not achieve the desired results. Let us not squander time to reach the target, which at times could be a pipe dream. The focus should be to improve and move on.

Eighty Percent of Tasks in Processes Are Waste

The author has seen that most of the steps in service processes are non-value-added. A lot of time is squandered in doing things that the customer will not be willing to pay for. On dissecting the process, it is usually found that 80 percent of the time is consumed by 20 percent of the activities. While applying lean principles for process improvement, the endeavor should be to eliminate or improve this 20 percent of the activities.

Time Is a Key Dimension of Lean

Some practitioners of improvement call lean *time-based management*. This is because one of the key objectives of lean is to take time out of processes. This is the reason why

	Date: _____	
Number	**Points**	**Yes/no**
1	The number of employees in the organization has been increasing in proportion to business volumes	
2	Each department within a business unit has their own management information system	
3	Chronic customer issues are erupting regularly	
4	There are individuals dedicated to work related to "reconciliation" or "rework" or "coordination" or "follow-up" or "exception management"	
5	Individuals in the workplace seem to be sitting idle	
6	Customers are waiting/spending a lot of time to get served by the organization	
7	The workplace looks very cluttered and disorganized	
8	The operating expenses of the company are going up in proportion to the increase in business volume, or volume is stagnant	
9	There are sofware applications that don't talk to each other	
10	The emphasis is on automation and applying information technology solutions to most process problems	
11	Process exceptions are a way of life in certain processes	
12	Despite a regular call center, customer contact center, or customer response center meant for the entire company, some of the departments have also set up their own individual customer response teams	
13	With every new product introduction, more processes are added despite commonalties in the process steps	
14	Any process has a large number of inspection points—makers, checkers, or auditors—to check the quality of processing.	
15	There are regular meetings to address interfunctional issues	
16	Similar reports are generated by a large number of individuals	
17	Help desks exist to address interdepartmental, process, or coordination issues	
18	Firefighting is a common phenomenon in the organization	
19	A process's steps are integrated in such a manner that they cannot be separated from the overall process architecture easily; they are not modular in nature, which would facilitate their easy removal	
20	The business has tightly-coupled, vertically-integrated value chains	
21	There is usually rework in process	
22	Incorrect sales leads are followed	
23	A large number of "hidden factories" exist	

Continued

Exhibit 1.1   Lean opportunity checklist: applicability of lean in the organization.

Continued

Number	Points	Yes/no
25	Processes require multiple signatures or approvals	
26	Promotional material reaches events after they are over	
27	New products are being launched without required support processes in place	
28	Excessive e-mail attachments and other "e-wastes"	
29	No process exists to manage server space	
30	Piles of inventory are occupying office floor	
31	Incomplete documents are being entered into the information technology system	
32	There are multiple hands-off in processes	
31	Nobody seems to "own" the customer	
32	The organization is not able to keep pace with the changing needs and expectations of its customers	
33	Standard processes do not exist in the organization, or even if they exist, they do not get followed	
34	Processes seem to be static and do not get improved	
35	Performance of processes is not measured and monitored	

Ver: 1

Exhibit 1.1   Lean opportunity checklist: applicability of lean in the organization.

time is used as a key measurement. To measure this dimension, *lead time of completion* is taken as the primary metric before and after the application of lean techniques.

Participation of the Entire Organization Across Hierarchy

A lean transformation is a people's movement. Successful execution requires that the entire organization participates in it. Implementation of lean involves people at all levels of the company. Everybody has a role. However, this varies with the organizational hierarchy and levels. As one moves up the organizational hierarchy, the role of the top management team is more directional and strategic in nature; members at the lower levels of the organization will have more hands-on involvement in improvements. It is imperative that roles at all levels of the organization in a lean transformation be clearly stated to avoid ambiguity. Also, ensure that both direct and indirect employees are involved. Indirect employees are associates who are not the employees of the organization but of partners.

Bias for Action

A key facet of lean transformation is bias for action. While working on an improvement project using lean principles, ensure that too much time is not squandered on planning and analysis. While doing improvements we often spend unreasonable amounts of time on planning and analysis. This has to be avoided. Planning and analysis has to be backed by quick action involving the participation of all relevant people.

Even the Best Processes Have Opportunities for Improvement

Despite having the best of processes, there is always an opportunity to eliminate waste in it. This is an important paradigm on which lean operates. It has often been observed that process owners will proclaim that they have great processes that do not require improvement. This is not true. The author has found that all processes deteriorate over a period of time and there is always an opportunity to reduce waste.

Customers May Also Create Waste in Processes

Service processes are generally manpower-intensive. Customers often provide the inputs to processes. Inputs could be information, data, documents, monies, and so on. They not only add variation to the process but also generate waste. For example, a customer filling out a home loan application form could provide incorrect or incomplete information that could subsequently create rework in the process.

To reduce customer-created wastes, companies have launched quite a few initiatives. One effective approach is allowing customers to serve themselves. For example, instead of a customer having to go to a retail bank branch for a home loan, the customer fills out a Web-based application and submits it for processing. This eliminates the problems associated with incorrect filling out of paper application forms by the customer services executive in the branch and the same having to reenter the data into an IT system.

Involve the Leaders in the First Few Lean Solution Development Efforts

While setting out on a lean journey, it is recommended that the top management team be involved in a few project improvements. Since getting their time for a long period may be a challenge, it is recommended that they participate in *lean breakthroughs*. This requires an investment of five or six days during which the leadership team members will get a hands-on experience in the power of lean. In the initial days of your lean journey, until the company gathers the capability to facilitate lean breakthroughs, the organization may require an outside expert who can facilitate this process. The power of lean breakthroughs is such that it converts even the doubters in the organization.

Processes Are Not Visible and Often Lack Ownership

Processes in service organizations are not visible. Unlike manufacturing companies wherein the processes are visible, in service companies process execution may not be visible before your eyes. This can present a challenge and make identification of waste difficult and arduous at times.

Processes often do not have "ownership" and can just be running without anyone really knowing who owns them. What is required are processes with end-to-end ownership. Visibility of processes can be attained by documenting the processes in detail and ensuring that there are measurements to track their performance on an ongoing basis. These metrics could be both lagging and leading measures.

Focus on Local Optimization Generates a Lot of Waste

Processes in service companies generally operate within organizational silos (see Figure 1.8). The objective of the teams who run the processes is to get the best result for their function without really looking at the impact they have on the outcome of the larger value stream. This local optimization leads to generation of lots of waste as each of the functions focus on different outcomes.

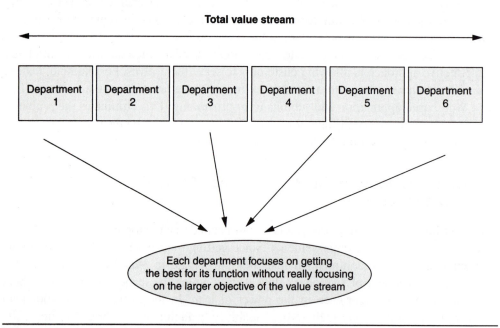

Figure 1.8   Local optimization creates waste within the value stream, as the focus of each of the departments is different.

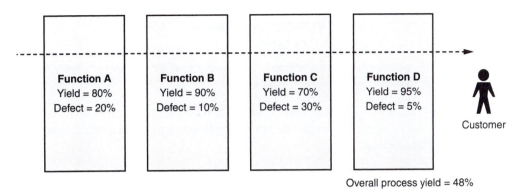

Figure 1.9 says: Overall process yield = 48%

Despite relatively high yields reported by the individual functions,
the total yield of the process is quite low.

Figure 1.9   Actual process yields versus functional yields.

Despite Low Defect Levels Reported By Individual Functions, the Value Stream Defect Levels Are Often Quite High

Due to the silo mind-set and focus on local optimization, the departments just measure the defects levels within their own function. The organization is quite content to see the low defect levels reported by each function. Little do they realize that the aggregated defect level at the value stream level is very high and this has negative impact on the customer. What is required is measuring the overall performance of the value stream and not just the function. The other way to put it is that the overall yield of the process could be much lower than assumed even though the individual silos may be reporting higher yields (see Figure 1.9).

Measurement Dichotomies Can Be Detrimental to Lean Transformation

The following are a list of measurement challenges that one often faces in service companies:

- Metrics do not give an end-to-end view of the processes. They just give the performance of the organizational silos.

- Metrics are not aligned to the strategic needs of the organization.

- Lack of standardized definitions and language of measurements, which does not allow comparison between business units. This also results in leaving the interpretation of metrics to individuals.

- Metrics often do not capture what the customer wants, rather focusing on what the company thinks to be important.

- Metrics largely ascertain the outputs and outcomes of the processes but do not help to predict them before they happen.

- Metrics do not help in taking actions. They are not real-time and not linked to the levers that will improve performance.

- Metrics are not user-friendly so that actions can be taken immediately. This is unlike a traffic signal where the colors red, yellow, and green clearly tell you when to take action.

All of the above shortcomings generate considerable waste in organizations and should be eliminated or avoided.

Improving Broken Processes Has Limited Impact

Focusing on improving broken processes will not deliver the desired impact. Create ownership for end-to-end processes (process loops) and work on improving them. Often, service organizations improve broken processes. Because of this the improvements do not positively impact the customer. For example, in a bank branch if there are issues pertaining to deliverables such as checkbooks, debit cards, or personal identification numbers (PIN) not reaching the customer on time, we should apply lean by looking at the process end to end, cutting across all functions. As you can see in the example in Figure 1.10, a customer walks into the branch to open an account. The branch couriers the application forms to the back office, which then couriers the deliverables to the customer. It should be noted that there are various functional owners for the activities in

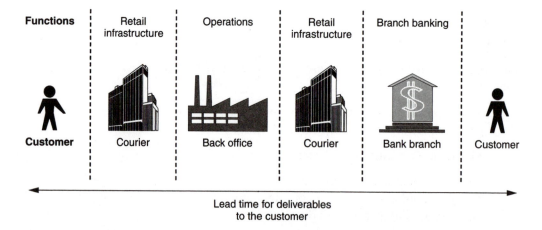

Figure 1.10 End-to-end process for resolving quality issues pertaining to deliverables not reaching the customer on time.

this process. The principles of lean should be applied to the entire process and solutions should facilitate management of hand-offs between the functions.

Service Processes Are Manpower-Intensive

Despite automation and technology interfaces, service processes continue to have employee interfaces. And wherever there are human touch-points in the process, the chance of errors increases. In such a case, managing the behaviors of the employees becomes extremely important. While technology does help in transactions such as the processing of papers or documents, providing the right experience to customers with the right interactions has become key for differentiation. As a result it has become key to ensure that employees are trained well and they are in a proper frame of mind that results in their making minimal errors.

So it is imperative that standard efficient processes get institutionalized in the organization. Remember, the customer experience comprises physical and emotional components. Physical components include attributes such as product quality, product range, price, accessibility, availability, time taken to serve, location of the outlet, channel used, and so on. Emotional components are how the customers feel and how their senses get stimulated. Organizations should plan to evoke the right emotions in the customers. So the message here is that just having efficient processes is not sufficient if they are not backed with desired emotions.

Workplace Organization Should Precede Transformation of Processes Through Lean

Waste gets hidden in disorganized workplaces. It is recommended that before an organization embarks on process improvements using lean principles, the workplace should be made free of clutter. This can be quite effectively achieved through an enterprise-wide implementation of 5S. While it is often believed that 5S can only be done in manufacturing companies, the author has made its unique application in service companies. Remember, improvement of a process in a clutter-free environment is much easier than in a disorganized workplace littered with files and paper.

Top Management Should Participate in Regular "Ground Zero" Walks

An integral facet of lean transformation is that leaders need to regularly do *ground zero walks*. This is to get a view of what is happening there. Ground zero refers to the place where the action happens in the organization. It refers to the workplace where the processes are run and where the customer encounters the process. A ground zero walk helps senior management to get to know the actual voice of the workplace. The entire top management team should regularly participate in such walks. Ground zero walks will be discussed in detail in Chapter 3, page 173.

A Platform of Standard Processes Is Foundational to Lean Improvements

Successfully sustaining lean in an organization requires a solid platform of standard processes. After improvements have been carried out, standard processes will ensure that new practices are followed until they become a part of the organizational and process DNA.

Standardization of processes has to happen at the following levels:

a. *Process.* This essentially refers to a set of interrelated activities that work in tandem to produce an output of value to the customer and help in accomplishing a business objective. For standardization to be accomplished, it is required that all the characteristics of a process are well defined and established. These have been listed and defined in Table 1.3.

b. *Procedures.* These are the "hows" of the steps in a process and specify how a process should get executed. The difference between a process and a procedure is shown in Figure 1.11 through the process adopted for making an egg omelet.

c. *Performance standards.* These are the specifications established from customer needs that the process should endeavor to meet.

The author has seen that wastes often are generated when the above have not been defined and established.

Some of the key lessons to remember are:

- The senior management team should lead the effort of defining and establishing processes. Processes should be defined by the senior management team, with the participation of members from the shop floor, workplace, or process.

- The teams from the shop floor or process should lead the effort of defining the procedures in a process.

Table 1.3 Characteristics of a process.

Number	Process	Definition
1	Purpose	The reason why a process exists in an organization
2	Objectives	The measure used to ascertain the effectiveness of a process
3	Inputs	Those items that enter the process and get converted into outputs
4	Outputs	These are the products or services that are the direct result of a process
5	Resource	Supplies that are used by a process when needed. They can either be used or consumed and comprise human, physical, or financial resources
6	Constraints	Anything that impedes the flow of a process; comprise things such as resources, regulatory guidelines, company policies, and so on

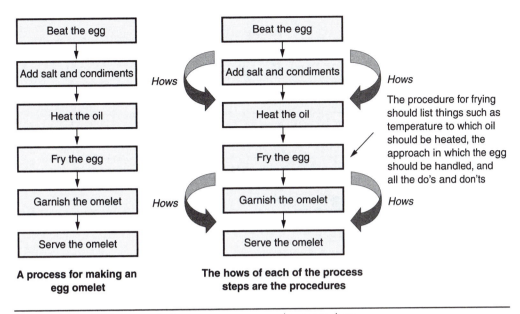

Figure 1.11 Differences between a process and a procedure.

- Identify the potential risks and the likely mitigators in all critical facets of processes controlled by regulatory and company policies in service companies.
- Leaders' and process associates' divergent views of processes should be reconciled.

Leaders' and Process Associates' Views of the Process— the Twain Shall Meet

It is surprising how different individuals' views of a process can be. While senior management looks at the process from the end-to-end perspective of the organization, the process associate confines their view to the activity that they handle in the process (Figure 1.12). As a result, both these constituents often do not appreciate the concerns that the other has for the process. In a lean transformation it is imperative that the process associate not only understand the challenges in their area of work but also appreciate the larger process issues pertaining to the end-to-end process and interdepartmental handoffs. Regular sessions should be held for the process associates to understand the big-picture process maps. Similarly, the top management team should make an effort to understand the challenges faced by the process associate while executing an activity.

Creating Flow Is Not Easy

In service processes, creating flow is often not easy. This is because processes are often not visible. Application of lean tools as used in the manufacturing world may not be possible. What is required is to intelligently adapt the solutions to the service sector without

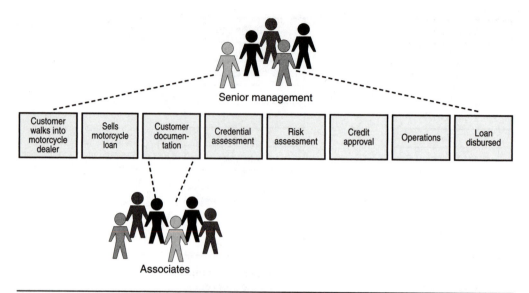

Figure 1.12   A vehicle finance disbursement process as viewed by top management and process associates.

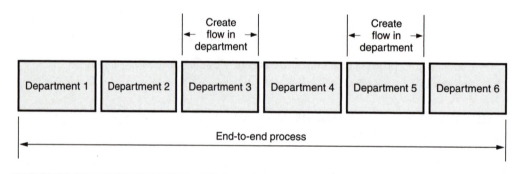

Figure 1.13   Approach to creating flow: first create flow within departments and then take it to the value stream.

losing sight of basic lean principles. Technology interfaces may be required when applying the principles of layout design, cellular manufacturing, and so on.

Gradually Create Flow in an End-to-End Process

Creating flow in an end-to-end service process should be done in a gradual manner. An end-to-end process often passes through a number of departments in an organization. The approach that should be followed is to first create flow within the departments and then thread them all together. For example (refer to Figure 1.13), if an end-to-end process encompasses six departments, the flow should first be created in the departments. Once this has been done and processes have been stabilized, we should look at expanding it to the entire end-to-end process. This is not easy and can sometimes take a lot of time if the processes do not first attain stability.

Create Geographical Cells

As the principles of lean are applied beyond the shop floor, there will be a need to apply the principles of layout design across geographies. This is especially true for organizations that operate in large geographies wherein the process travels a great distance, goes through multiple handoffs, and wades through multiple information failures. These processes not only demonstrate lack of ownership and ineffective inter-silo coordination but also lack a holistic view of performance. Such situations also can occur when the company has gone through a drive toward centralization and all the processing happens in a single or few locations. For example, Figure 1.14 shows the perils of centralization in an auto finance company. The focus on centralization has led to long travel times through the process and more process handoffs. An individual applying for a loan on the West Coast has to wait at least 10 days for their disbursement check. This is because the application must travel to centralized operations located 500 miles away to complete the disbursement process.

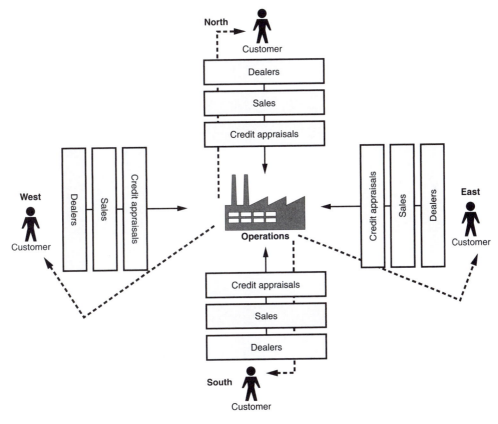

Figure 1.14 Centralization of operations in a financial services company.

With the objective of eliminating these problems, organizations can create geographical "cells" that radically improve process efficiency, customer service, and productivity.

Geographical cells are essentially end-to-end processes that operate within a defined region (Figure 1.15). Here, the constituents of the process are colocated and they operate in proximity to each other, leading to reduced handoffs. These processes have end-to-end ownership with a clear view of overall process performance. The implementation of the cell should be backed with a robust multi-skilling plan for the employees so that individuals can be moved laterally. Multiple geographical cells in a large country can also help in managing situations under adverse conditions and exigencies. This could be a part of the disaster recovery plan as one cell can stand in for another in case of emergencies.

Clearly State to the Employees That There Shall Be No Layoffs

As the organization commences with lean transformation and a large number of idle employees may be realized due to productivity and efficiency improvement, it is important that the organization have a plan in place to deploy them into some other role. If lean transformation leads to layoffs, the entire transformation will be derailed before it can fully take off. The top leadership should communicate at the very beginning of the transformation that lean transformation will not lead to any layoffs. Also, the human

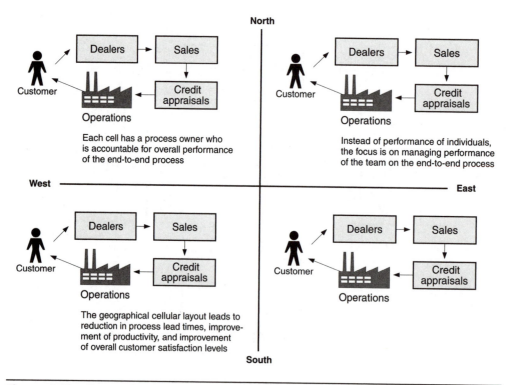

Figure 1.15 Geographical cells in an auto finance company.

resources department needs to play a role in ensuring that the feelings of the employees are managed well.

Leadership Needs to Be Patient

There are no magic wands in lean transformation. The initiative needs to organically grow within the firm before it can deliver full benefits. While there may be a few results that will be achieved instantly by process improvements, there are others that will take time. Leaders need to appreciate this. Making unrealistic demands for results could derail the entire transformation as employees may start taking shortcuts. Leadership will see results when the entire company gets involved in the transformation, and this will happen when employees have absorbed and assimilated the hows and whys of lean transformation.

Let the Workplace Communicate Through Visual Management

During lean implementation, leverage the power of visual management. Visual tools help to bring out the voice of the workplace and the processes. Such tools not only help to identify process impediments and abnormalities but also help in process flow. They also provide constant feedback on the process, not only helping to find process bottlenecks but also facilitating quick actions. They support the functioning of a lean management system in a workplace and help to bring life to the workplace. They also act as lodestars to improving the overall operational excellence of a workplace.

Focus on Multi-Skilling of Staff

In manufacturing organizations, multi-skilling is a key facet of effective functioning of the shop floor. However, in service companies the emphasis has been on specialization and achieving mastery over what an individual does in the workplace.

As a part of lean implementation, organizations need to ensure that employees are equipped with skills that allow them to perform a large number of activities. This requires that job responsibilities be expanded and shunning the dependence on a few people for ongoing activities. For example, in a retail bank branch there have traditionally been specialists for activities such as draft, cash, teller, customer service, and so on. This led to improper workload balancing. There would be instances when individuals were idle and the workload was not getting distributed among the staff members.

Multi-skilling helps to arrest this problem by tapping idle staff for performance of other operations and also by redeploying them during exigencies. It also helps to arrive at an optimal number in a workplace without allowing flab in manpower. Not to forget that it leads to creation of stand-ins for various roles. However, we should not confuse multi-skilling and multitasking. Multitasking is about an individual doing a large number of activities at a time. This should be discouraged as it generates a lot of inefficiency; often the individual starts a second activity before the first one is finished. This results in the pile-up of a large number of incomplete tasks.

To accomplish the above it helps if organizations carry out a skill inventory of all individuals (Table 1.4) and also publish a monthly skill summary dashboard (Table 1.5). These actions will move the overall skill curve of the business unit.

Application of Emerging Technologies to Bring in Efficiency

In the future, many emerging technologies will be used as a part of lean applications to enhance customer service, improve product availability, or provide superior operational efficiency.

Technologies such as biometrics, mobile banking, RFID (radio frequency identification) tags, grid computing, wireless access protocol, SIM (subscriber identity module) technologies, Java technologies, short messaging services, unstructured supplementary

Table 1.4 Skill inventory of employees.

Name	Skills											
	Financial analysis		Grooming		Selling		Product knowledge		Customer service		Presentation skills	
Jim Davis												
	1		1	2	1	2	1	2	1	2	1	2
Deb Cooper	4	3							4	3		
	1	2	1	2	1		1		1	2	1	2
Neena Jones		3							3			
	1	2	1		1	2	1		1	2	1	2
Trisha Sarkar					4	3			3		4	3
	1		1		2	1	1		1	2	1	2
David Jones									1	2		
	1		1		1		1		1			

Legend: Score of 4 = Master, Score of 3 = Expert, Score of 2 = Practicing, Score of 1 = Novice

Table 1.5 Skill summary: skill analysis of branch sales associates in a bank.

Type of skill	Novice	Practicing	Expert	Master
Financial analysis	20%	40%	40%	
Grooming	40%	30%	30%	
Selling	50%	30%	20%	
Product knowledge	50%	30%	10%	10%
Customer service	10%	50%	40%	
Presentation skills	20%	40%	10%	10%

services data, and grid computing are increasingly being used in service companies to foster operational excellence.

For example, RFID technology is being used for ensuring on-time availability of products. Wal-Mart has been using RFID on pallets and consignments to track them from suppliers' warehouses to their stores. RFID tags can be used to track food products from farm to plate. British retailer Marks and Spencer has been using RFID tags for men's suits, shirts, and ties to ensure 100 percent availability of their customers' chosen sizes, styles, and colors when they visit the store next time. Chase Bank in the United States has used RFID-enabled credit cards to facilitate quicker purchase of goods by waving the cards in front of point-of-sale terminals. ICICI Bank in India and First National Bank in South Africa provide their customers with mobile banking services to achieve greater efficiency and superior customer service.

Do Not Automate Waste-Laden Processes

One of the approaches adopted by some service organizations is that whenever there are process bottlenecks leading to long lead times, low productivity levels, or high defect levels, the solution implemented is process automation. This is the worst thing that can happen. The approach that organizations should take is to improve the process by removing waste. Once this is done, the process can be further improved by an information technology solution if required. Many times organizations adopt IT solutions to remove process problems that could just have been avoided. So automate processes only after wastes have been removed.

Metrics on Operational Excellence Not in Performance Scorecard

Metrics drive behavior. In many service companies the performance scorecards of individuals include objectives such as sales volume, number of calls made, transactions processed, and so on. It is unfortunate that they do not get evaluated on metrics that drive operational excellence such as process efficiency, customer service, cost efficiency, and so on. Without service fulfillment and cost-efficiency metrics, driving behaviors that facilitate lean thinking becomes impossible. For example, in call centers it has been observed that performance of associates is measured on talk time. The focus on talk-time minimization leads to the customer complaint or issue not getting resolved, which leads to repeat calls from customers and overall higher problem-resolution costs. The focus here should be problem resolution, even if it means greater talk time, to ensure that the customers do not call back on the same problem.

Oversight of Customer Interactions In a Process

Processes that are executed in service companies often have customer touch-points at various stages of the process execution. However, companies often do not have a clear view of the experience that the customers have at all these touch-points. Sometimes all that is done is to facilitate a customer survey once a quarter or once every six months or even once a year. The result of such a report does not add much of value to the organization except that the management gets to know that a customer satisfaction survey is being done. What is needed by organizations is to monitor the voice of the customer at each and every point of customer interaction. Companies serious about implementing a lean management system need to install listening posts at the places in the process where the customer is involved.

Apply Lean to Increase Revenue

Lean in service organizations also has a role to play in the revenue-enhancing processes. The lean intervention should not only bring about efficiency improvement but should also work toward improving the profitability of existing customers, enhance their "share of wallet," and facilitate acquisition of new customers. A lean management system should help increase the average financial return on existing customers, reduce costs to serve them, and increase the number of transactions by cross-selling new products or services.

Management Bandwidth Waste

It has been observed that in service companies decision making primarily rests with the senior management team. This not only results in process delays but also leads to the front-liners and process associates being ineffective at quick decision making, thereby leading to poorer customer service. Without empowerment and the authority to make decisions, these individuals, over a period of time, become robots, are de-skilled, and create unutilized capacity. Such a construct also leads to the senior executives spending time on issues that otherwise could have been delegated. As a part of LMS implementation, it is imperative that we look at the entire decision-making structure followed by the company. The endeavor should be to distribute the decision making across the organization and not just confine it to a few senior executives. To achieve this it is recommended that the entire company be trained on elementary problem-solving skills. Some organizations, such as the Ritz Carlton Company, even have a formal empowerment process.

Complexity Breeds Waste

One of the challenges that is being faced by organizations today is complexity in their operations. With the proliferation of products, services, channels, customer segments, business lines, and geographies, managing all these within the same business construct is not easy. A process that earlier only had to handle a few products, today is expected to process multiple products flowing through multiple channels while ensuring that the cost and efficiency levels do not deteriorate. Table 1.6 presents a list of product types in the global remittance business of a universal bank. Global remittance business is meant for individuals who work in a country other than their own and wish to remit their

Table 1.6 List of global remittance products offered by a major financial services company.

Types of Global Remittance Products	
Online	E-transfer
	Power transfer
	Cheque transfer
	Card based transfer
	Net express
	MeNRI
	NRI direct (online)
Offline	Speed transfer
	Insta transfer
	DD drawing
	NRI direct (branch based)
	Home point
	Wells Fargo (online option also available)
	Remittance card
	Easy receive account
Generic	Wire transfer
	FC cheque
	Outward remittances

earnings back to their home country. Just look at the number of product varieties that are being offered to customers!

Mass production techniques that were earlier applied for economies of scale may not always be relevant in such a situation. In addition, tougher regulatory requirements and increasing delivery standards of customers further add to complexity. Complexities add tremendously to processing costs across industries (see Figure 1.16). One of the primary reasons for complexity in business is the varying inputs and outputs of a process as against the standard design. Clearly, principles of lean can be very effective for reducing such problems.

Ensure That Employees Do What They Are Supposed to Do

In many organizations, employees spend a lot of time doing things that they are not supposed to do. This not only results in squandering of productive time but also generates a lot of inefficiencies, impacting overall product or service delivery. Following are some reasons why this happens:

- Lack of role clarity

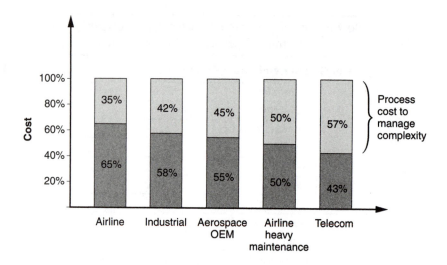

Figure 1.16 Cost of complexity as a percentage of operating cost.

Source: Hage et al., *Capturing Hidden Value: Eight Principles for Optimizing Processes* (McLean, VA: Booz Allen Hamilton, 2006).

- Being made to do things beyond current role
- Spending time to correct someone else's mess

Lack of Role Clarity

Often, individuals in organizations do not have a clear job description. Although individuals are hired for a specific role, their role has not been detailed. As a result, they are made to do a whole lot of things irrelevant to their central role. For example, a credit card sales executive spending time to ensure that a credit card gets delivered on time, which is not his role. His role should end with the customer filling out the application form. The delivery of the credit card is not his role but he does it because of lack of role clarity.

This is a problem that happens in companies who have to recruit a large number of employees in a short period of time. It occurs due to deficiencies in the recruitment process. How could one even think of hiring someone without having a proper job description? This typically happens when recruiting individuals for lower levels such as field salesmen, customer service representatives, relationship liason, and so on. Often, in a hurry to hire people, the recruitment process is completed without following the entire procedure. This can be disastrous. Little do these companies realize that many of these positions have customer-facing roles and can negatively impact the image of the organization if the right person does not get hired.

Being Made to Do Things Beyond Current Role

Despite having well-defined roles and responsibilities, an individual is often made to do things that he or she is not supposed to do. For example, a mortgage sales agent is told by his manager to look at resolving all customer complaints, which is beyond the scope of his current role. This should be avoided at all cost, and the responsibility to make this happen rests with the manager. It is the duty of leaders to ensure that their team members are not made to do things beyond what they are supposed to do.

Spending Time to Correct Someone Else's Mess

This is quite common when processes in an organization do not function in a flawless manner. As a result, the person who is next in the process has to clean up a mess that has been created by someone earlier in the process. For example, the sales executive for savings accounts in a bank who gets measured on the number of application forms that she receives, often submits customer application forms with incomplete documentation. As a result the credit appraisal executive has to follow up with the customer to complete the application documentation. This not only delays the process but also causes customer dissatisfaction, as the customer needs to be bothered for documents again. This can be avoided by changing the way the sales executive is measured. Instead of measuring her on "number of application forms," you can change it to "number of accounts opened" and "number of error-free application forms submitted." This would shift the responsibility to the shoulders of the sales executive.

A Day in the Life of an Individual

To root out the unwanted activities that are taken up by an individual and to find out what exactly an individual does during the day, the author has developed a tool called "A Day in the Life of _____." This is a simple exercise wherein the improvement team spends an entire day with an individual to see what he or she does. This tool serves the following objectives:

- Provides an overview of all that an individual does during the day

- Gives a feel for the time spent on nonnecessary work

- Helps to understand the challenges faced by an individual

- Helps to get an idea of whether there is clarity on the role

- Gives an overview on work overlap with other roles

- Provides a feel for possible work reallocation

- Provides clear opportunities for eliminating waste in current work

While carrying out this exercise, the activities of an individual get segregated as follows:

- *Necessary activities.* Work done as per the job description defined for the role

- *Unnecessary activities.* Work done by an individual that is not a part of the job description

Table 1.7   Example of an "A Day in the Life of _____" exercise.

A Day in the Life of a Customer Relationship Executive

Name of the employee: Tim James

Role: Customer relationship executive

Business unit: Branch sales   Location: _____

Time	Activities done	Necessary/ unnecessary	Remarks
9:00 – 9:15 AM	Switch on computer, attendance log-in	Necessary	Opportunity to reduce the time
9:15 – 9:45 AM	Morning meeting	Necessary	Can the duration be reduced?
9:45 – 11:00 AM	Telephone calls to potential customers	Necessary	
11:00 – 12:00 PM	Follow up on nonreceipt of customer deliverables	Unnecessary	This activity should be passed on to service executive and a team should work to eliminate this problem
12:00 – 1:00 PM	Lunch		
1:00 – 3:00 PM	Sales calls—visit new and existing customers	Necessary	
3:00 – 5:00 PM	Courier and mails to customers	Unnecessary	Should be passed on to the service executive
5:00 – 6:00 pm	Sales meeting	Necessary	Look at reducing the duration

A template that can be used for this purpose in shown in Table 1.7. The table shows an example of a role analysis of a relationship executive.

Don't Forget Customer Consumption

Lean is also about making the customer consumption processes efficient so that once they buy the product or service they are not faced with any hassles. Womack and Jones's latest book, *Lean Solutions: How Companies and Customers Can Create Value and Wealth Together,* provides insights into this dimension of lean. They have enunciated six principles of lean consumption:

- Solve my problem completely
- Don't waste my time
- Provide exactly what I want
- Deliver value where I want it
- Supply value when I want it

- Reduce the number of decisions I must make to solve my problems (Womack and Jones 2005)

I am not delving into the above as they are self-explanatory. However, for better clarity I would recommend that you consult their book.

For example, for a credit card issuing company, the relationship with the customer does not end with the issuing of the card. We all know the problems that one often faces when using a credit card. Until the company appreciates these concerns, I do not see the problems getting resolved. This is where analyzing the consumption process from the customers' point of view is critical. Companies should map out the customer consumption process and understand the places where it is likely to fail. Going forward, successful companies will be those who not only provide great products or services but also master the customer consumption process.

Lean Has Huge Application Potential in Public Services

The principles of lean have great potential for application in public services such as bus services, railways, education, healthcare, taxi services, airports, and so on. Many of these are run by government and do not get the attention required. Of course, a country such as Singapore is an exception, where a lot of effort has been made to provide better public services. Emerging economies, like India's, need to work toward achieving excellence in public services. There is a lot of untapped potential that is waiting to be harnessed. All that is required is the leadership will to make it happen. The opportunities for lean application in public services can be gauged from the simple checkout process (Figure 1.17) that a passenger has to follow after they land at a leading airport in India.

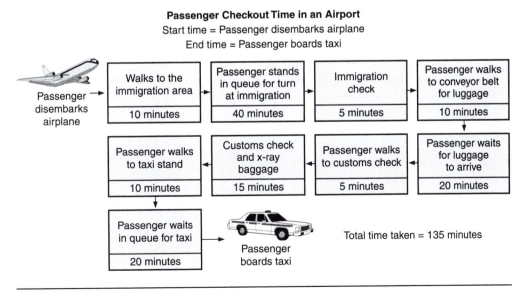

Figure 1.17 Checkout process from an airport in India.

The process starts at the time the airplane lands and ends when the passenger gets into a taxi. It takes a passenger more than two hours to get through the airport. Compare this with a similar process in an airport in Singapore. The author has personally seen that it takes only about 15 minutes to complete this process. In this example, the departments that need lean are baggage delivery, taxi services, immigration, and airport services.

Application and Documentation Processes Can Be Laden with Wastes

The documentation required for acquiring new business is often laden with a lot of waste. You may not realize that not only the organization but also their consumers may be made to generate waste.

The following are the two types of wastes that are often seen and can be eliminated with a little effort:

- *Size of the application document.* The size of the application document for many service providers such as cell phone carriers, banks, passport services, electrical or gas connection, and so on, is often quite large. Consumers are made to provide a lot of information in the application form that may either be redundant or not required. On making an inventory of the information that currently goes into an application form and ascertaining the objective that it serves, you will realize that a large amount of it is repetition and can be easily removed. While carrying out this process, do keep regulatory requirements in mind.

  In such waste-removal exercises carried out by the author, the size and/or number of pages in the application forms has been reduced anywhere from 40 percent to 60 percent for products such as auto finance or cell phone service.

- *Documents required as a part of the application process.* The other area in the application process that may be amenable to waste elimination is the number and type of documents required with the application form by the service providers. These documents act as testimonials and are required for meeting requirements such as identity, address, financial information, and so on.

  On probing as to why so many documents are required with the application form, the response that one typically gets from the users is that it is as per regulatory and policy requirements. Many times as policies and regulatory requirements change, documents get new information added without removing the obsolete information. Inadvertently, this results in the following:

  - Inconvenience to customers to provide information that may not really be required or is more than necessary

  - Avoidable work created for the processor as extra time needs to be spent on perusing the document

– Extra storage space; we all know that even two extra documents from each customer when added up can mean a lot of storage space

Exhibit 1.2 shows a template for weeding out unnecessary information from an application form.

Do Not Make Customers Produce Waste Because of Organizational Inefficiencies

There are instances when organizations make customers produce waste due to organizational inefficiencies, often resulting in customer inconvenience as well. Organizations need to be conscious of these inadvertent acts, which can severely impact customer loyalty. The following is an example wherein an organization makes customers produce waste.

Have you ever dealt with an organization that provides multiple services to customers? Each time you try to avail its services, you may have to go through the pain of providing your personal information again. This is despite the fact that basic customer information (such as name, address, passport time, social security number, and so on) is always the same. This is quite common in companies who provide a large number of products or services. For example, a company may be providing customers with multiple services such as telephone, cell phones, electric, gas services, insurance, and health services. When receiving services from each of these offerings, the customer has to fill out separate application forms despite dealing with the same company. This is extremely irritating to the customer as he or she has to fill out an application form for each of the products, resulting in a suboptimal service experience and customer dissatisfaction.

The organization is forcing the customer to create wastes because of its own inefficiencies. The solution to this is a common data-gathering mechanism in which the customer provides the information only once, which can then be used for all relationships and services that the company provides. This technology intervention radically reduces customer inconvenience. For subsequent relationships, the customer just needs to provide a unique customer ID. This is explained graphically in Figure 1.18.

Practice the Broken Windows Theory in Your Workplace

The broken windows theory was enunciated by James Wilson and George Kelling in their magnum opus *Fixing Broken Windows: Restoring Order and Reducing Crime in Our Communities*. The theory suggests that if a window is broken and left unrepaired, people walking by will conclude that no one is in charge and soon more windows will be broken, which could result in the anarchy spreading from the building to the street. The authors propound that a successful strategy to prevent vandalism is to start when the problem is small (Wilson and Kelling 1996).

I have seen the applicability of this theory in lean implementation. We cannot afford to overlook the small wastes in our workplaces and processes. When a piece of paper is not kept in the desired file and is left on your work table, very soon the whole table gets

Date: _____

Type of document: _____

Objective of the document: _____   Analyzing team members: _____

Policies governing the document:

1.

2.

3.

4.

5.

6.

Detailed information analysis:

Information	Objective	Type of information	Why required	Policy reference	Requirements as stipulated by the policy	Remarks

Decision table:

Type of information	Frequency of occurrence	Requirement as per policy/guideline	Difference	Action

Summary:

Attributes	Before	After	Remarks
Number of information			
Type of information			
Number of page			

Ver: 1

Exhibit 1.2   Template for finding wastes and redundancies in documents.

Before Lean Implementation

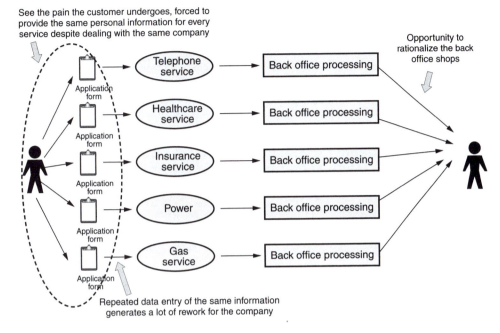

See the pain the customer undergoes, forced to
provide the same personal information for every
service despite dealing with the same company

Opportunity to
rationalize the back
office shops

Application form

Telephone service — Back office processing

Application form

Healthcare service — Back office processing

Application form

Insurance service — Back office processing

Application form

Power — Back office processing

Application form

Gas service — Back office processing

Repeated data entry of the same information
generates a lot of rework for the company

After Lean Implementation

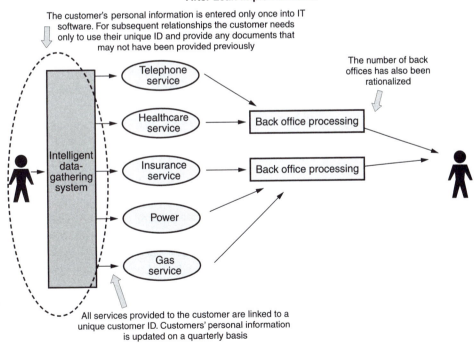

The customer's personal information is entered only once into IT
software. For subsequent relationships the customer needs
only to use their unique ID and provide any documents that
may not have been provided previously

The number of back
offices has also been
rationalized

Intelligent data-gathering system

Telephone service

Healthcare service — Back office processing

Insurance service — Back office processing

Power

Gas service

All services provided to the customer are linked to a
unique customer ID. Customers' personal information
is updated on a quarterly basis

Figure 1.18 Example of customer being forced to create waste and the associated customer dissatisfaction and pangs to the organization.

filled with other papers that have also not been kept in the proper files. One unkempt paper leads to another until the whole table is inundated with clutter. The same thing happens in processes. When one small redundancy is discovered in a process it should be immediately eliminated or else the whole process will soon become embedded with wastes. Whether it is a disorganized desk or a process laced with waste, if you see it you need to take action. Leaders at all levels need to remember that in a lean journey a large number of serious problems can be averted when we remove wastes. So even if there is a small problem that needs to be fixed, do not wait for the future. Go ahead and arrest it.

Engineer Speed, Quality, Flexibility, and Cost-Efficiency into Your Processes By Using the Principles of Componentization

While working on processes in service organizations it has been seen that creating flexible processes is very important. This needs to be done with the objective to create capabilities within processes to handle multiple products and reduce complexity. This is a concept that has been taken from the manufacturing world wherein common platforms, parts, and frames are shared among a number of product types and brands. For example, automobile companies have standardized components that they interchange to create different models. In a world of growing competition, when speed to market is critical, standardized operating platforms help to deliver new products to various customer segments in a cost-effective manner.

Let me give you two scenarios in which this principle can be used very effectively in your lean journey:

- *Processes made to handle multiple products and embedded with exceptions.* In service organizations, newer products get launched on short notice. As a result, the same process is expected to handle a large number of products, which not only makes the process complex but also embeds exceptions and work-around processes. If this doesn't work, newer processes are created to handle the new variances. This not only increases costs but also lead times and defects.

- *Outsourcing.* One of the ways to increase efficiency in organizations is by outsourcing components of the value stream to partners. However, this is not easy in tightly coupled value streams wherein separating the activities becomes difficult. The process of outsourcing will be easier in value streams that are modular, meaning they have been broken into activities or components that can be easily separated. Based on criticality and need, specific activities can then be outsourced.

This problem can very effectively be addressed through modularization of processes. This begins with breaking processes into the activities of which they are made up. This exercise is done for the processes of all products and services. The similar activities in all these processes are then aggregated and converted to independent modules or components, which are then used for all products. Organizations then create a basic construct of the modules wherein the modules are connected based on the given process or product. The results of this are that organizations benefit not by standardizing products but by standardizing activities or components that are shared across products or services.

Also, these modules act as Lego-like parts that can be combined into various permutations to create innovative products or services within a short period of time.

The clear benefits of modularization of processes are that it not only improves speed and quality but also reduces redundancies.

2
Blueprint for Implementation

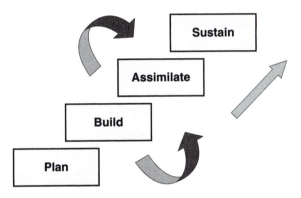

PLAN	Align	Leadership alignment
	Identify	Identify the value streams for product families
	Team	Form implementation team
	Define	Define implementation charter
	Configure	Configure the structure of the organization
	Install	Install anchors
	List	List all processes in the value stream

STEP 1: LEADERSHIP ALIGNMENT

The journey of implementing a lean management system should begin under the sponsorship of the chief executive officer. Without his or her buy-in, commencing an LMS journey will be futile. It is the CEO and only the CEO who can make the rollout of LMS successful. Before commencing an LMS implementation, the entire leadership team should be convinced that LMS is a business need and they will own its implementation.

The leadership team comprises the CEO and his or her direct reports. For a large multinational corporation, the leadership team comprises the following:

- Group chief executive
- CEOs of the business units
- Heads of corporate functions
  - Human resources
  - Technology
  - Strategy
  - Supply chain
  - Improvements

It is important for the leadership team to realize that successful LMS implementation requires it to be treated as one of the strategies for business success. Without a sense of urgency and its alignment with business strategy, an initiative like this can be quite time-consuming without delivering desired results.

The CEO should craft a compelling vision that clearly states the outcomes that are expected from LMS implementation. As the vision is created it is a good idea to revisit the mission and values that the company stands for. It is quite possible that these have undergone a change and require redefining in light of the new landscape that will be created through LMS. How will the organization's stakeholders such as customers, partners, and shareholders perceive us? The leadership team should also debate on the type of culture that will be needed to support LMS implementation. The endeavor should be built on a culture of customer-centricity, employee loyalty, and operational excellence.

Having defined the vision, the leadership team should clearly define the long-term and short-term outcomes expected from LMS implementation (Figure 2.1).

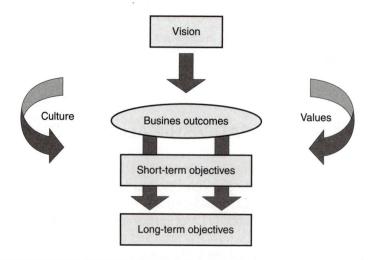

Figure 2.1 Vision, culture, values, objectives, and outcomes.

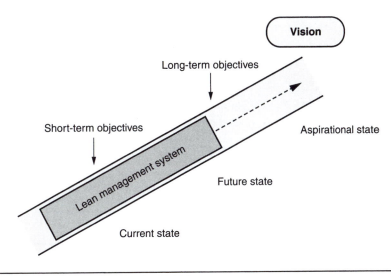

Figure 2.2 Role of objectives in the LMS journey.

Before setting out on a lean journey, it is imperative that the CEO and the leadership team list the metrics of relevant areas that will provide a holistic overview on progress. Metrics should cover both financial and nonfinancial outcomes. This should be scripted as current state versus future state and aspirational state (see Figure 2.2).

Assessment of Organizational Readiness

It is recommended that a quick assessment be done to ascertain the organization's readiness for a lean management system. Table 2.1 shows an assessment checklist that can be followed to determine a company's readiness for implementing a lean management system.

A basic prerequisite for LMS implementation is that all the points on the checklist in Table 2.1 be answered with a "yes." Even if there is a single "no" in response to the points, it is recommended that the LMS implementation should not be launched until it is corrected and you are sure that it will not have a negative impact on the organization. Otherwise, it would mean setting out on a journey for failure, which is something that an organization should never risk. It could mean losing the trust that the employees of an organization place in improvement. Note that the checklist focuses primarily on the CEO and the leadership team because they are the single biggest contributors to successful implementation.

The chief improvement officer should do this assessment. It has to be done by someone who catalyzes improvements centrally for the organization and has observed the functioning of the organization closely over the last few years. Remember, one may not get objective answers to all the points in the checklist, so an intelligent assessment is what is required.

Table 2.1 Organization's readiness assessment for implementation of lean management system.

Number	Process	Yes/No
1	Implementation of the lean management system will be treated as a business strategy for performance improvement	
2	The CEO will take up ownership of the LMS to make it successful in the organization	
3	Most of the direct reports will support the CEO's push for LMS implementation	
4	The CEO is convinced that LMS implementation will provide major competitive advantage to the organization	
5	There are chances of resistance from a few senior leaders but the CEO will be able to push LMS implementation through	
6	The CEO is seeking a drastic improvement in the way processes deliver results	
7	The CEO will spend time to monitor progress of the LMS implementation and subsequent sustainability	
8	The CEO will ensure that outcomes of LMS implementation are tied to the performance appraisal of relevant people in the senior management team	
9	The CEO intuitively believes that a lean management system will give him the most desired outcomes that will positively impact all of the company's stakeholders	
10	The CEO and the leadership team will spend time to get trained and understand what constitutes an LMS and what it takes to implement it	
11	The organization has been successful in most of the change management initiatives launched in the past	
12	There are no other major change initiatives under way in the company that will divert the attention of employees from LMS	
13	The CEO is looking at LMS implementation not just for quick results but for organic creation of a culture that builds "waste consciousness"	
14	The LMS implementation is not being looked as another cost-reduction program but as an approach to revenue enhancement	
15	The CEO will provide relevant financial support for LMS implementation	
16	The CEO will not only own LMS implementation but drive ownership down to all levels and ensure accountability for execution	
17	The CEO is willing to carry out the desired structural changes in the organization that are imperative to LMS implementation	
18	The CEO is looking at LMS implementation to reap long-term value for the organization	
19	To sustain the momentum of lean thinking, the CEO and leadership team will find ways to remind employees of the vision and outcomes that are expected from LMS	

Continued

Table 2.1 Organization's readiness assessment for implementation of lean management system. *(Continued)*

Number	Process	Yes/No
20	The CEO and the leadership team will state and ensure that there will be no layoffs as a result of LMS implementation	
21	The CEO will institute a group with the responsibility to manage the adaptive challenges that emerge due to LMS implementation	
22	The CEO and leadership team have a feel for the current problems faced with processes and customers	
23	The CEO and the leadership team will use all their influencing skills to catalyze execution	
24	The CEO and the leadership team will participate in a few lean breakthrough projects	
25	The CEO, head of human resources, and other leaders will take ownership of ascertaining the voice of employees who may not have authority and are low in the organizational hierarchy	
26	The CEO will ensure that LMS is implemented across the entire organization and its partners and not just confine it to a few departments or functions	
27	A member of the leadership team will sponsor all high-impact projects that are initiated under LMS implementation	

Lessons to Ponder . . .

The entire leadership team should focus its energies on making the implementation of the lean management system successful.

STEP 2: IDENTIFY VALUE STREAMS FOR PRODUCT FAMILIES

What Is a Value Stream?

The *Lean Lexicon* by Chet Markwinski and John Shook defines a value stream as "all of the actions, both value-creating and non-value-creating, required to bring a product from concept to launch and from order to delivery." It includes all steps involved in a product from initial concept until the money comes back to the organization from the customer. It comprises broad areas such as concept to launch, order to delivery, and order to cash. Remember, the value stream comprises all functions and stakeholders who need to work in sync for running the business of a product family.

The value stream is always identified with a product family. A product family refers to a group of products that broadly follow the same process steps. To identify the product family, use the product family matrix shown in Table 2.2. List all product lines in one column and list the corresponding process steps in the horizontal rows. Determine which products have similar process steps. This has to be done with an end-to-end perspective in mind, without forgetting any steps. This forms a product family that has a common path. Remember, the value stream for such product families should be considered when implementing process management.

As you can see in Table 2.2, product A and product F form a product family.

Further, at a conceptual level, a value stream has six blocks, which are as shown in Figure 2.3. Irrespective of the type of products or industry, all value streams follow the steps shown in Figure 2.3; whether consumer goods or financial products, they all follow these generic steps. While there can be a minor change in the sequence, the six blocks of the value stream will always exist in all business units. During lean management system deployment, teams work across these blocks to create efficient processes that deliver superlative performance.

Figure 2.4 shows the generic value stream of a mortgage finance business.

While this book is meant for the service sector, to clarify any misunderstanding: a similar value stream is drawn for a fast-moving consumer goods company such as chocolates, foods, or personal care products (See Figure 2.5). The order of the value stream blocks may vary but generically they are the same.

Table 2.2 Product family matrix.

Products	Process step 1	Process step 2	Process step 3	Process step 4	Process step 5	Process step 6
Product A	X		X	X		X
Product B	X	X			X	X
Product C	X			X		X
Product D	X		X	X		X
Product F	X	X	X	X		X
Product G		X	X		X	X

Product family

Figure 2.3 Generic value stream.

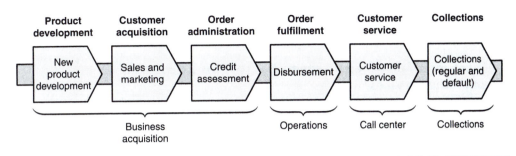

Figure 2.4 Generic value stream of a mortgage finance business.

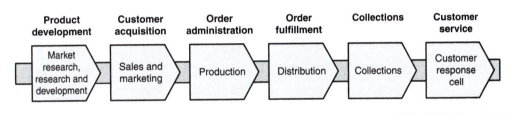

Figure 2.5 Generic value stream of a fast-moving consumer goods business.

When implementing LMS it is a must that it cuts across the entire value stream or else the desired impact from such an initiative will not be received. When LMS implementation is confined to a few functions, only part of the value stream is covered. As a result, the initiative does not deliver the desired impact. Organizations comfortably install lean processes in areas such as operations, customer service, collections, and so on. However, there are functions that are often considered not amenable to lean processes such as sales or marketing. Implementing a lean management system is about installing efficient processes across the value stream so that none of the functions are missed. The endeavor is to identify wastes across these blocks and take steps to reduce and eliminate them. Operational excellence is achieved when efficiencies are built into process loops, discussed later in this chapter in step 7. Despite these process loops cutting across functions and value stream blocks, the idea is to treat them as a single delivery platform with clear ownership. There are interface issues wherein handoffs need to be managed between the value stream blocks. Of course, this requires appointing an owner for the value stream and process loops, who takes ownership to ensure that performance happens, weave the value stream blocks, and install service-level agreements. We shall also be delving into these in detail later.

To summarize, identification of value streams for product families comprises the following:

- Listing all the products in a business

- Identifying the product families

- Identifying all value streams for each of the corresponding product families

What should be our approach if a business has a large number of product families?

In the case where a business has a large number of products and corresponding product families, you can prioritize the rollout. Begin by focusing on the vital few product families, those that make the maximum contribution to business volumes. However, it should be your endeavor to complete all the product families over a period of time. This is because a lean management system is about building efficient processes that exist in sync and work together for achieving the larger objectives of the business, and processes of one product family could be interdependent on processes of another product family. Also, there could be interaction among processes that are from different product families.

Lessons to Ponder . . .

Just installing ad hoc processes in a business is not sufficient. Get value from processes by implementing lean processes that cut across the entire value stream.

STEP 3: FORM IMPLEMENTATION TEAM

If efficient processes are foundational to an organization's journey to operational excellence, it is the people who make it happen. They are not just required for installation but also for ongoing maintenance of the LMS. They are the cast members who catalyze value extraction through the implementation of the lean management system and orchestrate a company's journey toward world-class. This is achieved through the following:

- By appointing individuals who can lead and facilitate building of a lean management system

- By identifying members who will hold the LMS "DNA" of a company

The following are the cast members who are an integral part of an LMS transformation:

- Value stream owner

- Chief improvement officer

- Lean maven

- Process paragon

- Process owner

- Lean navigators

- LMS managers

- LMS council

- Dashboard managers

- LMS assessors/process auditors

Value Stream Owner

The value stream owner is the person who has complete ownership of the value stream of a given product family. This individual is typically a senior person in the company who has the responsibility for the profit and loss numbers. A value stream could comprise more than one process loop.

The following are the roles expected of the value stream owner:

- Provides leadership to the entire value stream with responsibility for achieving the strategic business objectives

- Overall profit and loss responsibility for the product family

- Has ownership of development, processing, marketing, and sales of a select product family

- Leads the building of a lean management system across the value stream

- Ensures common alignment on the value-creating processes that make up the process loops

- Ensures that the process loops are managed to deliver business results

- Owns the implementation of LMS in the value stream

- Ensures that resources are deployed for flawless execution

- Facilitates smooth handoffs between functions

- Ensures that the performance of process loops is tracked

- Helps to remove barriers to execution

- Selects key process loops for improvement

- Owns, manages, and monitors all customers of the value stream

Chief Improvement Officer

The chief improvement officer champions the implementation of the lean management system in the organization. The chief improvement officer is a part of the organization's leadership team and directly reports to the chief executive officer. The chief improvement officer (CIO) is entrusted with the responsibility to catalyze all improvement activities of the organization. The CIO leads the LMS office and helps to promote the larger agenda of quality in the organization. He scripts the improvement road map and steers the larger journey of the organization toward world-class. He or she has a key role in building a culture of continual improvement and engaging the organization to adopt the agenda of improvement.

The following are the key roles of the chief improvement officer:

- Scripts the overall road map for LMS implementation

- Engages the CEO and others on the senior management team on LMS

- Works toward building a continual improvement culture

- Manages and catalyzes the entire change to LMS

- Acts as a coach for the CEO and the leadership team on LMS

- Helps the CEO, senior leadership team, and value stream owners to look at the relevant issues pertaining to LMS implementation

- Builds capabilities within the business to catalyze and sustain the LMS movement

- Installs the LMS anchors for sustainability of the lean management system

- Evangelizes the benefits of LMS to the organization

- Helps to import best practices from outside the organization

- Provides assurance to the CEO on the health of the lean management system after implementation

Lean Maven

These are individuals who are adept in the science of lean operations. The person has not only undergone formal training in the science of lean thinking but has also applied lean tools and techniques in improving processes. He or she acts as a technical resource on the science of lean thinking during implementation of the lean management system. The lean maven has the following roles in the implementation of LMS:

- Provides methodology and technical support during the implementation of LMS

- Helps the chief improvement officer to install anchors

- Facilitates leadership sessions for senior members of the value stream

- Creates change agents within value streams who will lead the lean management transformation

- Helps business leaders and value stream owners to develop lists of projects pertaining to their respective business group

What does it take to create a lean maven?

To qualify as a lean maven, an individual needs to do the following:

A. Undergo training covering a comprehensive body of knowledge. Learning should be ascertained through a qualifying test.

B. Lead to successful completion the following types of projects:

    1. Three projects pertaining to lean application on end-to-end value streams or process loops

    2. Three lean breakthrough projects

C. Successfully lead the deployment of a lean management system in a business or strategic business unit of an organization.

What should be the body of knowledge for a lean maven?

The following are the key topics that should be a part of the body of knowledge: lean thinking, Toyota Production System, concept of waste, value-added/non-value-added/business-value–added activities, value stream mapping, muda, mura, and muri, gemba kaizen, process management and standardization, just-in-time, push versus pull systems, lean supply chain, Kano model, lean consumption, agile operations, time-based competition, systems thinking, total productive maintenance, Six Sigma, Little's law, kanban, demand smoothing, cellular processing, inventory management, visual management, changeover reduction, theory of constraints, TRIZ, quality function deployment, concept screening, lean costing, lean product development, change management, performance measurement, balanced scorecard, fail-safing (poka-yoke), elements of services marketing, vendor teaming, statistical process control, pre-control charts, basics of project management, leadership elements, change management, lean product development, strategy deployment, A3 thinking.

What is the approximate duration required for completing the above body of knowledge?

It normally takes 20 to 24 days to complete the above program. It is up to organizations to complete the content in from two to four phases.

- Creates LMS councils within each value stream that oversee the implementation
- Works with value stream owners to develop action plans and spell out responsibility and accountability for their closure
- Helps in creating a project management architecture in each value stream
- Helps the value stream owners to review overall progress on an ongoing basis
- Reviews progress of projects implemented to improve specific process loops
- Coaches, trains, and mentors LMS project managers on their projects, tools, and conflict resolution
- Works with dashboard managers to set up measurement systems in value streams
- Runs a project management infrastructure to monitor progress of lean projects
- Communicates to teams the strategic power of lean management system deployment

The lean maven is a part of the LMS office. For effective implementation it is recommended that each value stream have a dedicated lean maven.

Process Paragon

This is an individual who understands the nuts and bolts of the process that are taken up for improvement during the implementation of the lean management system. This individual is a subject matter expert and knows the nuances of the process loops under scrutiny. For example, if a sanction process in a mortgage finance business is taken up for improvement, the process paragon will be an individual who has worked and knows the sanction process in detail. Typically, a process paragon learns the process through experience.

Process Owner

These are individuals who own process loops or end-to-end processes and have the authority to change them. They are typically senior management members who are responsible for facilitating design and rollout of processes. The appointment of process owners is dictated by the structure of the organization. In a functional organization, appointing process owners can be challenging. As a part of lean management system implementation, reconfiguring the organizational structure is critical and should not be avoided.

The key roles of a process owner are as follows:

- Helps to align the organizational objectives with customer needs
- Aids integrating the activities in a value stream
- Takes responsibility of the overall performance of the process

- Owns the expectations of the customer of the process loop

- Keeps tabs on the changing expectations of the consumer

- Steers the performance of the functional silos to ensure that the overall objectives of the process loops are met

- Facilitates installation of end-to-end metrics to aid the performance of processes

Ownership of process loops is critical; in many companies end-to-end processes do not have owners, which not only impacts performance but also is a source of organizational waste. With no end-to-end owner, neither are customer needs met nor are we able to ascertain their changing needs. The biggest benefit of end-to-end process ownership is that it avoids local optimization, instead concentrating on overall process performance.

Lean Navigators

These are individuals who get involved full-time in the implementation of the lean management system. Lean navigators are project managers who are selected from across the

Did You Know?

What are the specific qualities one should keep in mind while looking for potential lean navigators?

1. They should have high credibility in the organization or function where they work

2. They should have demonstrated a high level of competence

3. They should be acceptable to the employees

4. They should be able to see the big picture and see how the organization's priorities change over a period of time

5. They should have a sense of ownership of the organization

6. They should be assertive while not appearing intimidating

7. They should be able to articulate and carry forward the shared vision of lean management system implementation

8. They should have good communication skills and should be able to continually communicate the power of LMS, as well as goals, performance expectations, and feedback, to team members

9. They should have good problem-solving and team-building skills

What topics should be covered to prepare individuals as lean navigators?

The following are the key topics that need to be covered while preparing individuals as lean navigators:

1. Elements of lean thinking

2. Elements of lean consumption

3. Change management

4. Project management

5. Lean toolbox

6. Lean accounting

7. Systems thinking

8. Leadership elements

9. Strategy deployment

The above training program requires about 12 to 14 days.

What does it take to practice as a lean navigator?

To practice as an lean navigator, an individual needs to accomplish the following:

• Qualify with a written test.

• Demonstrate competence through on-the-job performance as a navigator for at least two months. If the person does not demonstrate the required competencies he or she may not be the right candidate for this role.

• Lead the successful completion of one lean breakthrough project.

organization to deploy the elements of the lean management system. These individuals work as catalysts of change and work full-time for a few years until the lean management system gets institutionalized within the company. Selecting the right candidates for this role is critical to the success of LMS implementation. The following is a list of points that need to be kept in mind while selecting candidates for this role:

- Target top performers from all functions such as sales, marketing, operations, technology, and so on

- Individuals need to be taken through rigorous training to assume this change management role

- Individuals will go back to their respective value streams to practice as navigators after they have undergone the required training

- LMS implementation requires individuals to be seconded to the role of navigators for a period of at least 18 to 24 months

LMS Managers

The LMS managers are individuals who run the management system that has been designed and implemented by the lean navigators. The LMS managers are typically the operating managers who are entrusted with the responsibility to run the processes and deliver the required business results. LMS managers include marketing managers, sales managers, product development managers, and so on. They include virtually all managers of the company who have the responsibility of executing the processes as defined. The LMS managers are responsible for running the processes on an ongoing basis and accountable for the performance of the local business system. For example, in a banking organization a branch manager who leads the operations of the branch is an LMS manager.

LMS Councils

This is the leadership team of the organization that provides directional guidance in implementing the lean management system. The LMS council exists at two levels:

- Corporate LMS council

- Value stream LMS council

The *corporate LMS council* is chaired by the chief executive officer and has his or her direct reports as members. The value stream owner chairs the *value stream LMS council* with his or her direct reports as members.

These leadership teams act as engines that oversee the design and implementation of lean management systems in the organization and the respective value streams.

To gain ownership of the entire leadership team, the CEOs of certain organizations rotate the chairmanship of the corporate LMS council among the members. The ownership for overall implementation of LMS within the company for a quarter is assumed by one of the leaders. Table 2.3 summarizes the key roles of a corporate LMS council and a value stream LMS council.

Table 2.3   Key roles of corporate and value stream LMS councils.

Number	Roles	Corporate LMS council	Value stream LMS council
1	Provide directional guidance to implementation teams	X	X
2	List the business outcomes expected from LMS for the organization and the value streams	X	X
3	Remove barriers to implementation	X	X
4	Finalize and validate the value-creating processes for the entire organization	X	
5	Finalize and validate the value-creating processes within each value stream		X
6	Decide on the key metrics that will be tracked to ascertain overall state of LMS implementation in the company	X	
7	Decide on the key metrics that will be tracked to ascertain the progress of LMS implementation in the value streams		X
8	Ensure that LMS implementation is treated as and integrated with business strategy	X	X
9	Continuously assess organizational culture, policies, and practices and how they are faring in the larger lean transformation	X	X
10	Drive out any fear that individuals may have about layoffs, and so on	X	X
11	Continuously communicate the overarching power of LMS and the values and beliefs that promote it	X	X
12	Identify value stream owners	X	
13	Identify process owners		X
14	Appoint dashboard manager	X	X
15	Support the installation of anchors for sustaining the gains from LMS implementation	X	X
16	Council member will spend at least one day per month on meeting and talking to customers	X	X

Dashboard Manager

As the LMS implementation gets under way, a dashboard manager is appointed to track key performance metrics. This person monitors performance areas such as people, processes, and business outcomes. This is to be done during implementation and continue after projects have been completed. The former is required to keep track of progress while the latter is done to ascertain the ongoing sustainability of deployment. Monitoring performance of completed projects is key as it prevents processes from going back to the pre-improvement state.

The dashboard managers operate at the following levels in the organization:

- Corporate dashboard manager

- Value stream dashboard manager

The corporate dashboard manager reports to the chief improvement officer while the value stream dashboard manager reports to the value stream owner. While the corporate dashboard manager is a full-time role, the value stream dashboard manager is a part-time role, which is executed in addition to the person's regular roles.

Both dashboard managers act as a voice to broadcast the performance of the lean management system throughout the organization. They alert senior leaders, value stream owners, and process owners to any exceptional circumstance in a timely manner. They ensure that dashboards are prepared within stipulated time frames and that the information is used to arrive at root causes. Whenever there are deviations, they make it a point to summarize the impact of the same on the business objectives and results. The corporate dashboard manager also works with the organization in devising a policy on what data are to be made freely accessible and what should be restricted.

During the early days of LMS implementation, the dashboard managers can commence implementing dashboards manually and then graduate to partial automation. But his or her ultimate goal should be computerization, which ultimately enables automation of the processes for data entry, analysis, and reporting. This not only increases efficiency but also reduces errors. Digital dashboards (also called cockpits) allow timely access of LMS metrics by key stakeholders.

The dashboard managers should have an information technology background and should have a liking for data. A word of caution here is that setting up digital cockpits is often not easy. This is because many of the processes may be manual and automating them may require enormous resources. Other challenges are that data systems often do not talk to each other and a lack of standardization of measurement systems across the company.

LMS Assessors/Process Auditors

These are individuals who carry out the assessment of the lean management system and processes. You will get an idea of the roles that these people play after going through the Audits section in Chapter 3.

Lessons to Ponder . . .

The types of decisions taken up by the LMS council will decide the quality of LMS implementation in an organization.

STEP 4: FIRM UP THE IMPLEMENTATION CHARTER

Having decided to go on a lean transformation journey, there is a need to put in place a charter for implementation. This document is scripted by the senior leaders and acts as a guide during implementation. As Stephen Covey has said: "Begin with the end in mind." (Covey 1992). The charter clearly states the business benefits expected from the lean management system *before* one sets out on an implementation journey.

So, What Is an Implementation Charter?

An implementation charter is a document that states an organization's commitment to embark on a lean transformation journey. The charter gives an overview of all the work that will be required to build a lean management system. This document is fairly comprehensive in nature and details all information pertaining to the business that will be relevant during implementation.

This document forces top management to think through all issues before putting an enterprise's resources to work on processes. Separate charters should be prepared for the entire organization and the respective value streams.

The corporate LMS charter (Exhibit 2.1) should be signed by the chief executive officer, chief improvement officer, and the CEO's other direct reports. The value stream owner and his or her direct reports should sign off on the respective value stream charters.

The charter should clearly state the benefits that are expected from the implementation of the lean management system. Experience shows that without clear objectives, implementation of LMS can be an academic exercise and may not deliver the required benefits to business. The charter helps to align the implementation plan, processes, and strategic business objectives.

The corporate LMS charter should be scripted by the chief improvement officer in the presence of the CEO and other council members. The finalized charter should be formally signed off on by the CEO and all of his or her direct reports who are members of the council.

Similarly, the value stream owner should create the LMS charter for his or her value stream in the presence of the other council members. This document should also be signed off on by all members of the council.

Getting the signatures may appear to be ritualistic but it drives ownership among all the leaders. Even the most reluctant of the leaders will doubly make sure that he or she understands what is required for LMS implementation. It is recommended that copies of the corporate implementation charter be shared with all employees and even displayed at all workplaces to act as visual reminders.

To summarize, the benefits of the charter are as follows:

- Provides a directional road map for implementation of the lean management system in the organization

Date: _____

Lean Management System
Corporate Implementation Charter

Date: Charter no.:

Organization/company targeted: _____

LMS vision: _____

Reason for adopting LMS:

Current business pains:

Current business opportunities:

LMS objectives
    1. Customers:
    2. Financial:
    3. Process:
    4. People:
    5. Capabilities:
    6. Others:

Business goals:

Business goals	Year 1	Year 2	Year 3	Year 4	Year 5
Customers					
Financial results					
Process					
People					
Capabilities					
Others					

Business groups:

Business units	Turnover	Major product families	Major value streams	Business objectives	LMS objectives

Continued

Exhibit 2.1   Template of charter for LMS implementation in an organization having multiple value streams (as adopted in a financial services business).

Continued

LMS council members:

    Chair:

    Members:

Key cast members for implementation:

Business units	Business head	Value streams	Value stream owners	Lean maven	LMS navigators

How will success be measured?:

Critical success factors for implementation:

Anticipated challenges in implementation:

Signed: Chief executive   Chief improvement officer

Signature of other members of corporate LMS council:

1: _____ 2: _____ 3: _____

4: _____ 5: _____ 6: _____

Ver: 1

Exhibit 2.1 Template of charter for LMS implementation in an organization having multiple value streams (as adopted in a financial services business).

- Provides a business case for LMS implementation and the impact on business objectives
- Lists all the key cast members in the LMS implementation
- Helps to get buy-in and commitment from the entire leadership team
- Lists all the likely challenges and possible mitigants
- Including the CFO as a part of the charter helps in independent validation of benefits
- The process of charter preparation brings out the likely resistance among the leadership team—this helps the CEO to take proactive actions to convert such individuals

---

Date: _____

Lean Management System
Value Stream Implementation Charter

Date: Charter no.:

Value stream:

Value stream owner:

Product families covered by the value stream:

Reason for starting an LMS journey:

Current business pains:

Business opportunities:

LMS objectives
   1. Customers:
   2. Financial:
   3. Process:
   4. People:
   5. Capabilities:
   6. Others:

Business goals:

Business goals	Year 1	Year 2	Year 3	Year 4	Year 5
Customers					
Financial results					
Process					
People					
Capabilities					
Others					

Objectives:

Value stream:

   Where does it start?:

   Where does it end?:

   Vendors/outsourced partners in the value stream:

Value stream LMS council:

   Chair:

   Members:

Continued

Exhibit 2.2   Template of LMS charter for a value stream.

Continued

					Start date	Closure date

Implementation team:

    LMS navigators:

    LMS managers:

    Lean maven:

Project ownership details:

Project names	Responsibility	Accountability	Consultation	Information	Start date	Closure date

Likely investments:

Critical success factors for implementation:

Anticipated challenges in implementation:

Signed: Value stream owner   Lean maven

Signature of other members of corporate LMS council:

1: _____ 2: _____ 3: _____

4: _____ 5: _____ 6: _____

Ver: 1

Exhibit 2.2   Template of LMS charter for a value stream.

Did You Know?

Do not hasten the preparation of implementation charters. It is quite normal to have a few meetings before it takes final shape. Be patient. Remember, hurrying at this stage can be detrimental to subsequent implementation.

Lessons to Ponder . . .

The CEO has to get involved in scripting the implementation charter. His or her involvement level will be an indication of how important he or she sees this initiative for the success of the organization.

STEP 5: REDESIGN THE STRUCTURE OF THE ORGANIZATION

A prerequisite for LMS implementation is that the organizational structure be reconfigured to facilitate achievement of desired strategic business objectives. Without this modification, the desired results from LMS can be a mirage. This is a major realignment of the organization and brings about a change in the way the company functions. The following are the key facets of the new organizational design:

- Organization is structured around product families or value streams catering to specific market segments

- Individuals take complete ownership of the performance of value streams

- Value streams act as business units and have all required functions within them

- Value-creating processes have well-defined ownership

- Overall performance of the enterprise is the amalgamation of the performance of the individual process loops within the value streams

- Aligns organizational objectives with customer expectations and needs

- Cost and process efficiencies are achieved from leaders being able to control resources

- Focus on minimizing wastes and the associated costs generated due to coordination among functions

- Endeavors to reduce the complexities of managing a large organization, which requires more leadership oversight and higher inter-function coordination costs

- Creates small autonomous business units within the company through value stream ownership—this creates leaders and a leadership bench within the company

- Targets meeting current and changing customer needs by linking the front end, back end, and business partners

- Brings in greater accountability to serve the customer and achieve operational excellence

- Facilitates faster decision making, and the corporate LMS council or the top management are closer to performing value streams (or business)

- Projects are taken up by project managers with an objective to deliver benefits to the entire value stream

Figure 2.6 shows the typical structure of an organization structured around value streams.

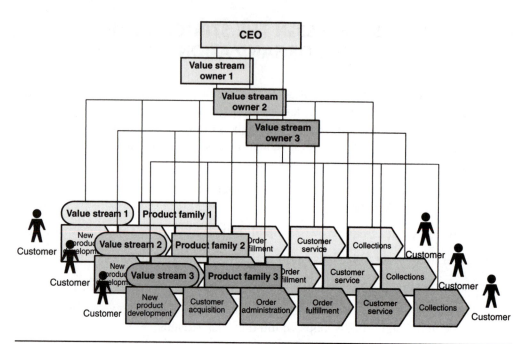

Figure 2.6   Organizational structure for lean management system implementation.

As can be seen in Figure 2.6, each of the value streams are independent entities that have all the capabilities and resources to manage a product family. Each of the value streams has all the required functions within itself such as product development, marketing, sales, collections, and customer service. These value streams serve specific market segments. This makes the organization nimble and able to respond to the needs of the market at great speed. Whether it is the time spent to design and launch a new product or the time taken to respond to customer needs, overall organizational velocity improves drastically. This model makes even a large organization as agile as a small company.

A structure based around value streams ensures horizontal integration of processes that cut across functional silos. Unlike a functional organization wherein efforts are targeted toward achieving functional excellence, in an organization structured around value streams the efforts are targeted toward achieving excellence across the value stream. This structure arrests local optimization in a functional silo and facilitates optimization across the value stream.

Each of the value streams is owned and led by individuals called *value stream owners*. The value stream owner is responsible for the overall performance of the value stream. The value stream owner is a part of the top management team and reports to the chief executive officer or an individual one or two levels below him or her. The value stream owner is the business head responsible for the profit and loss of a product family. The value stream owner also catalyzes operational excellence and simultaneously focuses on customer convenience, profitability, customer retention, new business acquisition, and cost efficiency.

Performance Management and the Value Stream

The realigned organizational structure requires a change in the way performance is managed in the organization. Traditionally, the focus was on bettering the performance of each function even if it meant impacting the expectations and needs of the customer. In the reconfigured structure the enterprise goals are broken down into respective value stream goals. These value stream goals are further broken down into goals for the respective blocks (or functions) of the value streams (see Figure 2.7). The overall accountability for the value stream rests with the value stream owner, and each of the value stream blocks or functions contribute to make it happen. The performance management of all individuals in the value stream is targeted toward overall organizational performance excellence and not their respective functional excellence.

Organizational Structure for Lean Management System

Figure 2.8 shows the overall organizational structure of an enterprise required for LMS implementation. Together with value stream owners, the corporate functions directly report to the chief executive officer. Each of the value streams are independent business units and have all resources within them necessary to run a business. Many of the corporate functions are strategic groups having skeletal staff that support the CEO on key issues that impact the functioning of the organization. Each of these departments are also present in the respective value streams.

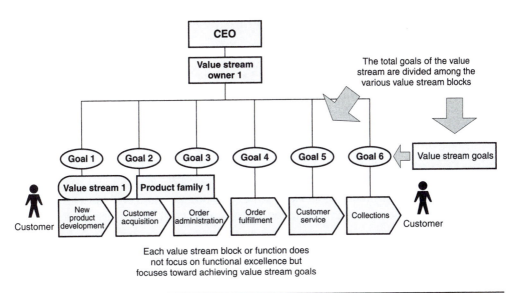

Figure 2.7   Process of goal decomposition in an organization structured around value streams.

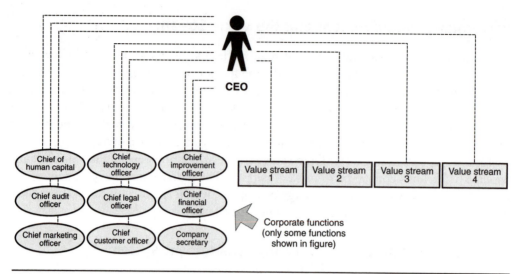

Figure 2.8   Organizational structure necessary for LMS implementation.

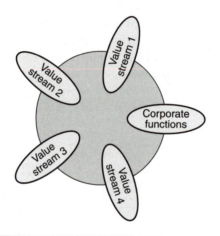

Figure 2.9   The "firm within a firm"—value streams as independent entities.

Value Streams and Customer Segments

An organization structured around value streams is often termed a "firm within a firm" as each of the value streams function independently and cater to specific market segments (Figure 2.9). Each of the value streams has profit and loss responsibility.

Let's examine a bank that underwent this structural change. Before their journey of lean transformation, this retail bank had been structured around products (see Figure 2.10).

This resulted in the same customer being approached by multiple representatives of the bank. This often resulted in the bank not being able to design products based on the needs of the customer. This led to customer dissatisfaction impacting customer loyalty.

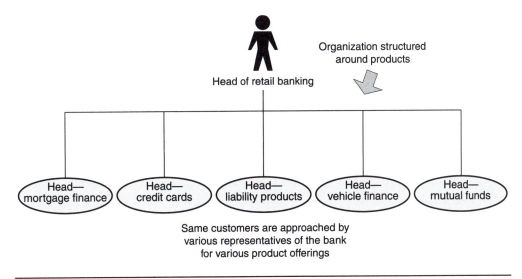

Figure 2.10   Structure of retail bank before commencing the journey of lean transformation.

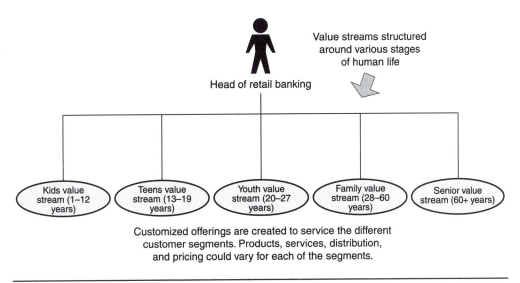

Figure 2.11   Value streams crafted around specific customer segments.

Also, it generated a lot of waste as a lot of processes had to be repeated for each of the products.

As part of their lean transformation, this retail bank decided to institute an organizational structure with value streams targeted to customers at various stages of their life (see Figure 2.11). Based on the customer segment (life stage of an individual), specific offerings are designed comprising product, service, pricing, and distribution channel. Each of the value streams offers an array of products geared to the specific customer segment. And the value stream owners have profit and loss responsibility. This differentiated approach to customer service not only helps to serve customers better but also garners their loyalty. And remember, loyal customers will not only recommend the organization to others but may also increase their share of business with the company.

Lessons to Ponder . . .

The organizational structure portrays the power, priorities, and strategies of the company and how serious it is about LMS implementation.

STEP 6: INSTALL ANCHORS

Anchors are the building blocks that support the architecture of a lean management system. They are individuals, infrastructure pillars, processes, entities, and behaviors that support the implementation and sustainability of the lean management system.

This is a key step in the journey of building a lean management system in an organization. The anchors provide the required wherewithal to fulfill the organization's strategy of LMS deployment. While the organization structure provides the basic construct of the company, the anchors are the levers that translate strategy into results. This is shown in Figure 2.12.

I call the anchors the "five P's of the lean management system" and they are the following:

- People
- Processes

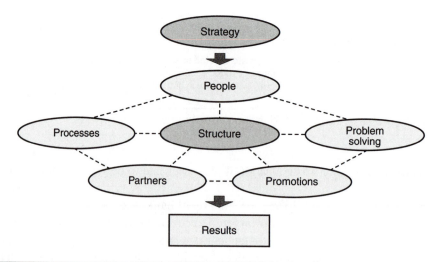

Figure 2.12 The five P's of the lean management system.

- Partners

- Promotions

- Problem solving

The five anchors are closely linked and work in tandem as a chain (see Figure 2.13) to deliver the expected results. A single missing link can impede the successful implementation of the lean management system.

The five anchors are further detailed in Table 2.4.

Figure 2.13 The lean management system chain.

Table 2.4 Functions of the five anchors in a lean management system.

People	Processes	Partners	Problem solving	Promotions
Value stream owner	Management reviews	Process partners	Large improvement projects	Rewards and recognition
Chief improvement officer	Knowledge repository	Vendors	Small improvement projects	Problem prevention mind-set
Lean maven	Audits		Improvement vault	Brown bag sessions
Process paragon	Performance management			A3 promotion
Process owner	Meetings			Value stream thinking
Lean navigators	Ground zero walks			
LMS managers	Daily meetings			
LMS council				
Dashboard manager				
Chief customer officer				
The customers' cell				
LMS office				
Help desk				
LMS marketing manager				
Human resources department				

The following are the key reasons why anchors are required in a lean management system:

- Build the foundation for a lean transformation

- Help in implementation and sustaining of the lean management system

- Provide the skills and mind-sets to implement LMS

- Reward the right behaviors that provide positive results

- List the key cast members in lean implementation

- Keep the engine of continual improvement moving in an organization

- Create capabilities for ongoing sustainability

- Endeavor to make lean thinking an integral part of the organizational fabric

- Create moorings that support the continuous quest for operational excellence

The details of anchors are discussed in Chapter 3, so are not being discussed here.

Lessons to Ponder . . .

Anchors are "moorings" in a lean management system that support the organizational quest for operational excellence.

STEP 7: LIST ALL PROCESSES IN THE VALUE STREAM

Inventorying the processes in an organization and its respective value streams is an important step in the implementation of a lean management system. I have seen service companies wherein a lot of inefficiencies are generated because the management does not have a structured approach to managing the operations in the organization. Employees do not know which processes are core to the success of the business nor what role they play in its being able to deliver results. Also, as new products are created, new processes are also created. Managing the processes becomes difficult as the constellation of processes expands. If this happens in a disorganized fashion it can spill over into major customer issues and impede the smooth functioning of the processes.

One of the philosophies that drives LMS implementation is continually getting back to the basics. So begin by listing all the processes that operate within the organization. This should be done even if a company has a good regimen of managing the processes, as it will cause the processes to be looked at through a critical lens. Before this is discussed, we will revisit the types of processes that operate in a firm.

Any organization has broadly four types of processes:

1. *Value-creating processes.* These are those processes of an organization that directly (a) help in achievement of business results, (b) contribute to customer satisfaction, and (c) facilitate output delivery.

2. *Value-enabling processes.* These are processes that work closely with value-creating processes but do not directly impact business results, customer satisfaction, and output delivery.

3. *Support processes.* These are processes that support the value-creating and value-enabling processes of an organization. Typically, they are similar across the organization and cut across functional silos and strategic business units.

4. *Management processes.* These are the processes that help to hold the above processes together by making them function in a flawless manner. They help in the governance and maintenance of a process management framework.

See Table 2.5 for examples of the four types of processes as found in a mortgage finance business.

The relationship between the four types of processes is shown in Figure 2.14.

As a part of LMS implementation, begin by working on the value-creating processes. Instead of wasting time on all the processes, the endeavor is to focus on the vital few processes that are strategically important to the firm. Remember, when we are talking of value-creating processes, we are talking about end-to-end processes that can stand by themselves and have a definite start and end point.

The value-creating processes may vary according to the type of business. Table 2.6 shows the value-creating processes of a few businesses in which the author has worked.

Table 2.5 Examples of value-creating, value-enabling, support, and management processes of a mortgage finance business.

Number	Value-creating processes	Value-enabling processes	Support processes	Management processes
1	Business acquisition	Market research	Recruitment	Corporate governance
2	Credit assessment	Lead management	Infrastructure management	Management reviews
3	Disbursement		Information technology	Assurance
4	Customer service		Payment	Document management
5	Product development			Compliance
6	Collections			

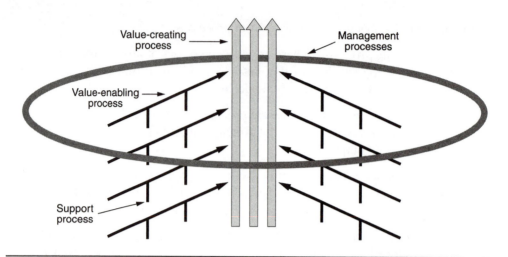

Figure 2.14 Relationship between value-creating, value-enabling, support, and management processes.

Table 2.6 List of value-creating processes in various types of businesses.

Number	Auto finance business	Ice cream business	Universal bank	Hair oil manufacturer
1	Sales	Product development	Business acquisition	Marketing
2	Credit administration	Distribution	Credit and risk management	Supply chain
3	Product innovation	Customer service	Technology	Distribution
4	Customer service	Corporate governance	Customer service	Product development
5	Collections		Collections	

Value-Creating Processes and Key Process Loops

The value-creating processes typically form what we call *key process loops* (KPLs) in a value stream. There are multiple process loops in a value stream. A prerequisite for consistent performance by a value stream requires that the KPLs function flawlessly in unison. A single broken key process loop can derail the performance of the value stream, impacting the overall performance of the business. I call them "process loops" as they "loop" together in unison to deliver results.

Like conducting an orchestra, all the process loops in any organization must be managed effectively. This requires that leaders translate business goals into process terms across all functions.

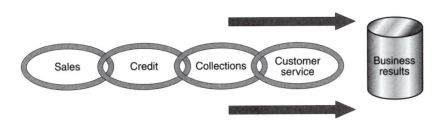

Figure 2.15 Key process loops of a value stream.

As part of LMS implementation, list all the organization's process loops and ensure that their flawless functioning is on the radar of management. Typically, the outputs and outcomes of key process loops will be the deliverables of senior leaders such as value stream owners, the top management team, and CEO.

Based on the type of business, the number and type of process loops in a value stream may vary.

Lessons to Ponder . . .

Value-creating processes are the strategic assets of an organization.

BUILD	Learn	Build relevant capabilities
	Select	Select the value stream on which you want to focus
	Ensure	Ensure that all the stakeholders in the value stream are on board
	Ascertain	Ascertain what the customer values and requires
	Map	Map the current state and baseline the process
	Visualize	Visualize the future state
	Dissect	Dissect and carry out detailed process analysis
	Deploy	Deploy lean solutions

STEP 8: BUILD RELEVANT CAPABILITIES

Capability-building is a key facet of lean management system implementation. It is required not only for implementation but also for subsequent sustainability. In the beginning of the journey, the organization could outsource capability development to a third party. However, within a certain period of time the organization should ensure that the required capabilities are created in-house to deliver the programs on an ongoing basis.

Table 2.7   List of key capability-building programs required for the implementation of a lean management system.

Awareness programs	Leadership programs	Technical programs	Certification programs	People programs
Lean Management System and Me	The Leadership Alignment Session	The LMS Workshop	The Lean Maven Program	Change Management for Lean
Lean Thinking	The LMS Estimation Sessions	The Process Workshop	LMS Assessor's Certification Program	Managing Teams in a Lean Environment
Seeing the Unseen: The Wastes of Lean	Lean Management System: An Enabler for Business Performance	Advanced Lean Tools Workshop	Train the Trainer for the LMS Workshop	
The Tool Box: Lean Tools We All Should Know	Strategy Deployment Workshop	LMS Assessment	Train the Trainer on Value Stream Mapping	
Path to Lean Management System	A3 Thinking	Benefits Quantification and Lean Accounting Workshop	Train the Trainer for the Process Workshop	
Elementary Problem Solving		Lean Breakthrough Experience	The LMS Navigator's Workshop	
		LMS Offices— How to Create	Process Auditor's Program	
		Value Stream Mapping		
		Managing for Continual Improvement		
		Problem Solving for Lean		
		Lean Product Development		

LMS implementation requires an effective capability-building infrastructure. The value stream corporate councils take ownership of capability-building and regularly review its progress. The chief executive officer also reviews the overall progress during the corporate LMS councils.

Capability-building for LMS implementation requires that the following training programs be delivered to the organization:

1. *Awareness programs.* These programs are targeted toward creating awareness among the employees of the company and endeavor to demystify "why we are doing what we are doing."

2. *Leadership programs.* Leadership programs are required for getting the alignment and buy-in of the leadership team.

3. *Technical programs.* These programs are targeted toward building specific capabilities for subsequent application.

4. *Certification programs.* These programs are targeted to validate the specific capabilities possessed by an individual. Certification programs provide an assurance of the abilities of individuals.

5. *People programs.* These programs are targeted toward managing the "people" dimensions of lean implementation. They specifically endeavor to create support systems that produce a motivated and passionate workforce who live the organizational values.

Details of each of these training programs are listed in Table 2.8.

Table 2.8 Details of capability-building training programs.

Program type	Program name	Program objective/ description	Duration	Target audience
Awareness	Lean Management System and Me	Provides details on what a lean management system is and how it helps an individual to achieve the larger organizational objectives	8 hours or 1 day	All employees
Awareness	Lean Thinking	Provides an overview on the fundamentals of lean thinking and how to create a mind-set of continual improvement and lean thinking	8 hours or 1 day	All employees
Awareness	Seeing the Unseen: The Wastes of Lean	Gives insight into the various types of wastes and how one identifies them in one's workplace	8 hours or 1 day	All employees
Technical	The Toolbox: Lean Tools We All Should Know	Instructs participants on the basic tools and techniques for carrying out improvements in a workplace	2 days	LMS managers, select employees
Awareness	Path to Lean Management System	Examines what it takes to implement a lean management system in a company	4 hours	All employees

Continued

Table 2.8 Details of capability-building training programs. *(Continued)*

Program type	Program name	Program objective/ description	Duration	Target audience
Technical	Elementary Problem Solving	Equips individuals with the process to lead and facilitate improvements in one's workplace	2 days	All employees
Leadership	Leadership Alignment Session	Provides leaders with an overview of the lean management system and how it can facilitate achievement of strategic objectives	1 day	Leadership team (CEO, functional heads, business heads, value stream owners, process owners)
Leadership	Strategy Deployment Workshop	Based on Toyota's *hoshin* planning process, the program teaches leaders how to align functions and activities with strategic goals of the company	2 days	CEO, functional heads, business heads, value stream owners, process owners
Leadership	LMS Estimation Session	Session targeted to brainstorm and list all the projects to be taken up that will help in achieving the strategic objectives of the organization. The outcome of this session is the list of projects and the likely benefits that they will deliver to the company	1 day	CEO and direct reports, business heads/value stream owners, and direct reports
Leadership	Lean Management System: An Enabler for Business Performance	Provides details on the lean management system, its various components, and the cause-and-effect relationships among them	1 day	CEO, functional heads, value stream owners
Technical	LMS Workshop	Provides details of the hands-on nitty-gritty of lean management system implementation	1 Day	Process paragon, process owner, LMS managers, dashboard managers
Technical	The Process Workshop	Provides the basics of the science of business process management and how it helps to achieve business objectives	2 days	Process paragon, process owner, LMS managers, dashboard managers
Technical	Advanced Lean Tools Workshop	Equips participants with all the tools required for carrying out improvements using lean in a company	2 days	Lean navigators
Technical	LMS Assessment Workshop	Creates competencies for understanding the assessment process of the lean management system	2 days	LMS assessors

Continued

Table 2.8 Details of capability-building training programs. *(Continued)*

Program type	Program name	Program objective/ description	Duration	Target audience
Technical	Benefits Quantification and Lean Accounting Workshop	Acquaints participants with methods for capturing benefits from a lean project and the approach to be followed for accounting in a lean organization	2 days	CFO's team members, lean navigators
Technical	Lean Breakthrough Experience	Gives a firsthand overview of what it takes to carry out a lean breakthrough in a short period of time and the benefits reaped	5 days	Leadership team, value stream owners, functional heads, lean navigators
Technical	LMS Office	Provides details on the wherewithal required for maintaining an LMS office and how to make it be an effective force in lean transformation	2 days	Lean navigators, lean mavens, members of LMS office
Technical	Value Stream Mapping	Explains the technique of value stream mapping and how it can be used to identify wastes	2 days	Lean navigators, LMS managers, dashboard managers
People	Managing for Continual Improvement	Provides all the "do's" for creating, managing, and monitoring a continual improvement culture in a company	2 days	Value Stream owner, LMS managers
Technical	Problem Solving for Lean	Equips participants with the "choose to close" approach to improvements	3 days	Lean navigators, LMS managers
Certification	Lean Maven Program	Creates experts in the science of lean operations	24 days	Individuals chosen to provide expertise to lean transformation
Certification	LMS Assessor's Certification Program	Create assessors who can carry out assessment of the lean management system	3 days	Selected individuals
Certification	Train the Trainer for LMS Workshop	Create trainers for running the LMS Workshop	3 days	Selected individuals
Certification	Train the Trainer for the Process Workshop	Create trainers for running the Process Workshop	3 days	Selected individuals

Continued

Table 2.8   Details of capability-building training programs. *(Continued)*

Program type	Program name	Program objective/ description	Duration	Target audience
Certification	Train the Trainer for Value Stream Mapping	Create trainers for running value stream mapping workshops	3 days	Selected Individuals
Certification	The Lean Navigator's Program	Create change agents who can facilitate lean transformation	14 days	Lean navigators
Certification	Process Auditor's Program	Create auditors for carrying out process audits	2 days	Potential process auditors
People	Change Management for Lean	Provides the "hows" to managing change in an organization during a lean transformation	2 days	Functional heads, value stream owners, LMS managers, process owners
People	Managing Teams in a Lean Environment	Provides the critical success factors for improving the effectiveness of teams in a lean journey	2 days	LMS managers, process owners
Technical	A3 Thinking	Equips participants with A3 thinking related to A3 problem solving and A3 strategy deployment	2 days	Team leaders, business heads, functional heads, process owners, value stream owners
Technical	Lean Product Development	Teaches participants the lean product development process and targets maximum knowledge growth with reduced lead times	3 days	Product development managers, marketing managers, value stream owners, innovation managers

Responsibility of LMS Capability-Building

The onus of building capabilities should rest with the individual value streams and business units. Each of the value stream owners and business heads should take it upon themselves to ensure that the capabilities are built as desired. This is quite different from the model wherein the ownership of training rests with a corporate or central training team that resides within the human resources department and their representatives run the training programs.

In LMS implementation, the LMS office accepts ownership of developing the technical content and creating resources within value streams that can further reinforce the training programs.

The Role of the LMS Office in Capability-Building

The following are the roles to be played by the LMS office in capability-building for LMS:

- Catalyzes capability-building for the lean management system by providing all required support for training delivery

- Works with the value streams and business units to create resources for training delivery

- Builds content and develops various channels for training delivery

- Retains in-house specialists who provide subject matter expertise on training topics

- Certifies the training and capability-building competencies of resources within values streams and business units

- Gets outside expertise on topics on which the organization and lean management office do not have capability

- Facilitates outsourcing of training delivery whenever required; maintains strict control on the quality of the outsourced agency hired

- Ensures a check on the quality of training delivered by trainers within functions and value streams

- Keeps track of the training programs delivered by trainers of the value streams; helps to calculate the overall training person days

- Installs training processes for smooth delivery of training programs pertaining to LMS

- Maintains and runs the training infrastructure of the company

- Prepares monthly dashboard on the overall capability status of the company and the respective value streams

- Integrates the larger capability-building needs of the company in its journey toward the lean management system

- Provides feedback to business and value stream leadership on the quality of the capability that is being built

The approach taken by the LMS office to building relevant capabilities is shown in Figure 2.16. The focus is to create trained resources within value streams and functions that further take responsibility for capability-building in their respective areas. Remember, the accountability for capability-building rests with the value streams and not the LMS office.

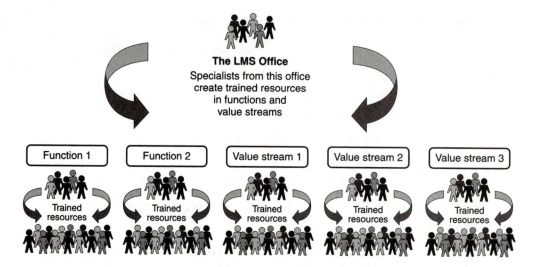

Figure 2.16   Approach for capability-building rollout during LMS implementation.

Awareness Programs

It should be a primary endeavor to touch all employees with the awareness programs. These are a must as each employee in the organization needs to know why the journey of lean management system was undertaken and how it benefits their work and the organization. I have seen companies take the awareness programs lightly and look at them more as something they have to do as compliance. It is recommended that a senior resource within the value stream take ownership of awareness programs. This individual will not only manage the awareness creation but will be accountable to ensure that all employees get touched by all the awareness programs listed in Table 2.6. While the awareness infrastructure can be run by the LMS office, the execution must be by the individual who has the responsibility to make in happen within the value stream. Web-based training can be leveraged here and will be discussed in detail in the next section. Also, it should be ensured that awareness programs do not just become a one-time exercise. The focus should be on repeated reinforcement.

Web-Based Learning for the Lean Management System

While on the journey of LMS implementation, it is recommended that you leverage Web-based resources for training delivery. It is not only cost-effective but has a large number of benefits that traditional classroom training does not provide. It facilitates learning in times and places where traditional training is not possible.

The following is a list of benefits provided by Web-based training:

- Allows individuals to learn from their respective workplaces

- Provides access to training materials 24/7

- Allows you to reach a large number of people— especially beneficial to companies that are scattered over far-flung geographies

- Facilitates learning at a pace that is suitable to the learner

- Helps to instantly ascertain the learning of the trainee

- Training program is less intimidating as trainees do not run the risk of being "exposed"

- Highly cost-efficient as expenses pertaining to travel, high-cost facilities, and so on, are eliminated

- Delivery of training is consistent for all recipients

- Allows easy updating of latest information into the training content

- Tracks attendance of employees who have taken the training program

- A quiz at the end of the session helps to ascertain the employee learning

Some people have shown concern about the effectiveness of Web-based training. This is unfounded, as a study conducted on learners in the United States has shown that Web-based training is as effective as classroom training. For details I recommend that you see the work done by William Horton and Tammy Whalen.

A lot of emphasis should be placed on capability-building of employees in the lean journey. Any shortcuts here can be very detrimental. Leaders cannot outsource this activity to others. If they are serious about lean, they have to own it and make it happen.

 Lessons to Ponder . . .

- Taking a shortcut in capability-building is committing *hara kiri* in the journey of lean transformation.

- In the first stages of a lean implementation, it makes sense to hire an external expert to guide the organization. This not only helps reduce the learning curve but also helps to instill the right practices. Yes, hiring a good expert is key.

STEP 9: SELECT THE VALUE STREAM ON WHICH YOU WANT TO FOCUS

After all the value streams have been listed, an organization may decide to prioritize and not focus on all of them at the same time. The prioritization of the value streams could be based on parameters such as their impact on the overall organization's strategic business objectives (assuming that the company has a large number of product families and corresponding value streams) and the various voices discussed under Problem Solving in Chapter 3.

Having prioritized the value streams, the focus should be to work on the processes that show opportunity for improvement.

Typically, the processes to be selected would be dependent on related business pain and the requirements of the organization. Business pains include issues pertaining to consumers, regulators, people, or financial numbers that are currently of concern to the organization. The source of these pains are various voices such as the voice of the customer, voice of the regulator, voice of the process, voice of the partners, voice of the shareholders, and so on. Business needs include proactive intervention in a process to take performance to the next level. For example, a process may be improved to take customer satisfaction to best-in-class.

In the initial phases of LMS implementation, the focus should be on the value-creating processes to arrest issues of concern to an organization and also to facilitate proactive improvements. Examples of value-creating processes were shown in Table 2.6.

As a rule of thumb, among the value-creating processes, take up the process that has the maximum opportunity for improvement. Value stream mapping should be done for this process.

Lessons to Ponder . . .

Instead of commencing with lean implementation across the entire enterprise, you may decide to begin with a business unit or small area of the organization and target to completely transform it. The benefits should be so visible that they create a pull among the other employees.

STEP 10: ENSURE THAT ALL STAKEHOLDERS OF THE VALUE STREAM ARE ON BOARD

Identifying stakeholders is imperative before commencing on a lean transformation. Often lean efforts fail because all stakeholders are not involved in the transformation and their subsequent support during implementation of solutions is weak. As experienced by the author, identifying all stakeholders of organizations having multiple value streams is often not easy. There are often instances when important constituents are missed who contribute to the execution of the process. Remember, these stakeholders could be within or outside the organization. *Value stream stakeholder analysis* is a mechanism to help list all the stakeholders that directly and indirectly contribute to the performance of a value stream. This analysis is a strategic exercise and requires the presence and participation of the entire leadership team associated with a product family.

The author has developed and successfully employed a tool called the *value stream stakeholder matrix* (VSSM), which facilitates in stakeholder analysis before a lean transformation.

What Is a Value Stream Stakeholder Matrix?

This tool is used to identify and list all the stakeholders who impact a value stream and contribute to its overall performance. The following are the key benefits of a value stream stakeholder matrix analysis:

- Listing of all stakeholders who impact a value stream

- Ensuring that all the stakeholders cutting across functions are included in end-to-end process management

- Seeking buy-in of all the constituents impacted by a process change

- Finding the handoffs between the departments and functions

- Facilitating value stream transformation

- Installing service-level agreements to track and monitor the performance of the constituents

Types of Stakeholders in a Value Stream

Stakeholders impacting a process could be of the following types:

- *Principal stakeholders belonging to the company.* These are constituents who are not only a part of the process flow but also a part of the organization.

  An example of a principal stakeholder belonging to the company is the operations function in the sanction process of a mortgage business.

- *Principal stakeholders not belonging to the company.* These are constituents who are a part of the process flow but not a part of the organization. They could be entities such as vendors, outsourced agencies, or direct marketing agencies.

  An example of a principal stakeholder not belonging to the company is a direct marketing agency used to acquire business for an auto finance company.

- *Enabling stakeholders belonging to the company.* These are constituents who are not a part of the process flow but are a part of the organization. These constituents, though not a part of the process, support the functioning and execution of the process.

  An example of an enabling stakeholder belonging to the company is the retail infrastructure department for supporting the selection and maintenance of branches of a liability business in a bank.

- *Enabling stakeholders not belonging to the company.* These are constituents who are not a part of the process flow and do not belong to the organization but support the functioning and execution of the process.

  An example of an enabling stakeholder not belonging to the company is the IT support provided by a vendor to help run the sanction process in a mortgage business.

The following are the steps to be followed when doing a value stream stakeholder analysis of a product family. For clarity, the example of a value stream stakeholder analysis of an auto finance business is discussed together with each of the steps.

Step 1

Get all of the following members into a room:

- The chief executive officer or the business head who is the value stream owner

- Heads of the key functions of the value stream such as sales, marketing, production, customer service, and so on

- Heads of corporate functions such as the managers of improvements, technology, human resources, and so on

- Lean maven—A technical expert on the value stream management

- Process owners—All the individuals who own the value-creating processes in the value stream

- Lean navigators—These are change agents who are responsible for catalyzing change in the value stream.

Step 2

List the generic steps of a value stream.

As you know, a generic value stream typically has six elements. Irrespective of the type of business that an organization is in, they all follow the configuration shown in Figure 2.17.

Step 3

List the elements relevant to your business corresponding to the six generic value stream elements. Name the elements as they are commonly known in the business. As shown in

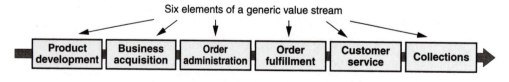

Figure 2.17   Elements of a generic value stream.

the example in Figure 2.18, the value stream elements of an auto finance business comprise product and policy, sales and marketing, credit administration, operations, customer service, and collections.

Step 4

Under each of the VSM elements, list all the principal stakeholders. They are the constituents who are a part of the process flow for executing the jobs pertaining to each of the elements. These constituents could be within or outside the organization. In the example of an auto finance business (see Figure 2.19), the constituents involved in the element titled *product and policy* are departments such as policy, risk, legal, technology, product, and operations. There may also be constituents outside the organization such as field investigation (under the element of credit administration) that have been outsourced to an external firm.

Step 5

Now list the enabling stakeholders. These are those constituents that are not a part of the process flow but support the performance of the process or value stream. Again, these

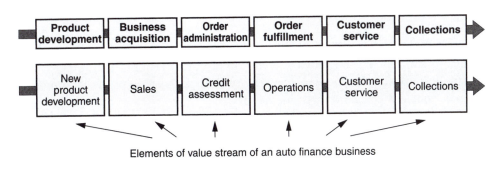

Elements of value stream of an auto finance business

Figure 2.18   Value stream elements of an auto finance business.

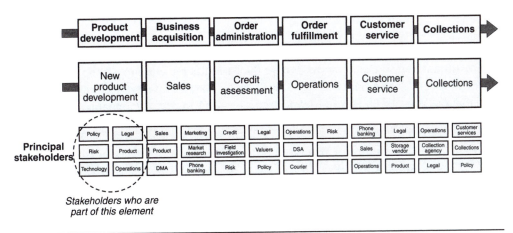

Figure 2.19   Principal stakeholders in a value stream of an auto finance business.

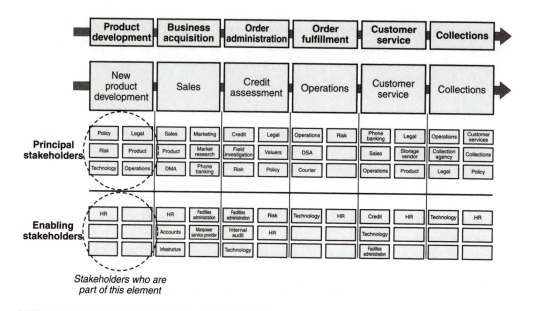

Figure 2.20   Principal and enabling stakeholders in a value stream of an auto finance business.

could be within or outside the organization. In the auto finance example (see Figure 2.20) one of the enabling stakeholders is human resources (HR), which is under all the elements. In this example, HR is an enabling stakeholder as it helps in recruitment and training of people who execute and run the process.

Step 6

After the stakeholders have been listed in the boxes as shown in Figure 2.20, the team should clearly identify the four types of the stakeholders, that is: (1) principal stakeholders (belonging to the company), (2) principal stakeholders (not belonging to the company), (3) enabling stakeholders (belonging to the company) and (4) enabling stakeholders (not belonging to the company). Shade each of the four types of stakeholders in four different colors (see Figure 2.21).

The value stream stakeholder matrix gives a pictorial overview of the stakeholders of a value stream. It also clearly shows where the handoffs are that need to be managed for flawless process execution within a value stream. The VSS matrix has universal application across industries. Beyond lean, it can be used in any organizationwide change initiative.

Lessons to Ponder . . .

Missing the stakeholders during a lean transformation can derail the entire journey.

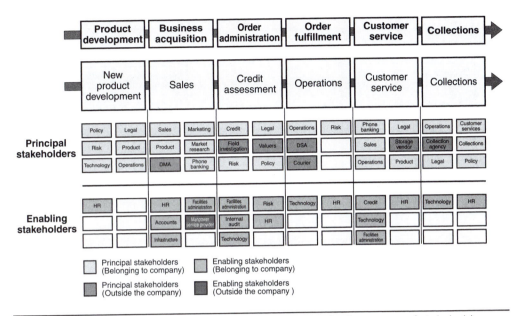

Figure 2.21   Value stream stakeholder matrix showing the four types of stakeholders.

STEP 11: ASCERTAIN WHAT THE CUSTOMER VALUES AND REQUIRES

Having short-listed the process, there is a need to identify the customers of the process and what they value and require. This is imperative given the fact that the final improvements have to be targeted toward meeting the requirements of the customer. Remember, this has to be accomplished before commencing with value stream mapping.

While there are a number of approaches to ascertaining customer requirements, I have personally found the SIPOC-R diagram to be quite handy. When read backward, from right to left, SIPOC-R, stands for requirements, customer, output, process, input, supplier (see Figure 2.22).

To complete the SIPOC-R diagram we begin by defining the requirements of the customer. These should be listed in the box headed "requirements." List the customers of the process in the box titled "customer" and the outputs that these customers need in the box titled "output". The suppliers and the inputs to the processes should be listed the boxes titled "supplier" and "input" respectively. In the area labeled "process" list the macro process steps of the process for which the value stream mapping needs to be done.

The following are the primary reasons for using the SIPOC-R diagram:

1. Helps to ascertain the requirements of the customer

2. Gives an overview of the macro process steps in the process

3. Listing of suppliers and inputs ensures that nothing is forgotten when the value stream mapping is actually done

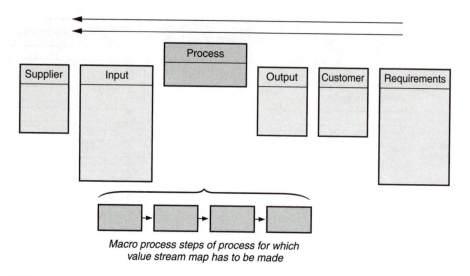

Figure 2.22   Example of a SIPOC–R diagram.

"Used" versus "consumed" process inputs

When listing the inputs of the process, focus on "inputs" that are both "used" as well as "consumed." Inputs labeled as "consumed" are those that are transformed in the process while inputs labeled as "used" are those that are used in the process but are not transformed themselves. Examples of items that are consumed are documents, raw materials, and so on, while items that are used include people, equipment, and so on. Remember, the items that are used also get consumed, but over a long period of time.

"Helicopter view" of the process helps in SIPOC-R

Before doing the SIPOC-R diagram it helps to take a "helicopter view" of the process. This will help you to determine the macro process steps of the process. A helicopter view is accomplished by doing a quick process walkthrough and listing the major activities that happen in the process. Do not confuse a detailed process walkthrough with a helicopter view of the process. The former is a detailed study of a process wherein you capture all the relevant data and information, while the latter is a quick overview of what goes on in the process.

Figure 2.23 shows an example of a SIPOC-R diagram that was done before commencing with value stream mapping. The process pertains to a motorcycle finance company.

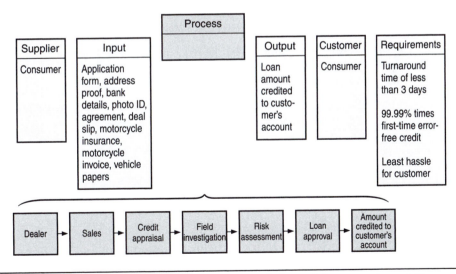

Figure 2.23   Example of a SIPOC-R for a motorcycle loan disbursement process.

Did You Know?

Customer is not just the end customer

Customer thinking in lean is not just about meeting and satisfying the requirements of the end customer (also called the "consumer") but also about meeting the needs and requirements of the next person in the process. This can only be achieved when the walls between departments, work areas, and operations are broken down. Whenever there is a problem in a process, individuals cutting across functions or departments must come together to solve the problem. Customer thinking is at times about losing on departmental or functional goals in order to meet the larger goals of the process or value stream.

Did You Know?

The five steps of lean transformation

Womack and Jones came up with a five-step approach for lean transformation in 1996. It comprises the following:

1. Specify value from the standpoint of the customer

2. Identify the value stream for the product family

3. Introduce flow—arrange steps in tight sequence

4. Let the customer pull value from the next upstream activity

5. Strive for the perfect process

Please note that the approach to the lean management system as specified in this book is built on the above principles (Womack and Jones 1996).

Lessons to Ponder . . .

Embarking on a lean project without understanding what the customer wants is like shooting in the dark. Bring precision to your projects by aligning them with customers' needs.

STEP 12: MAP THE CURRENT STATE AND BASELINE THE PROCESS

In the implementation of lean, processes have to be looked at from two levels:

1. From 10,000 feet

2. From five feet

The View from 10,000 feet

Looking at processes from 10,000 feet means getting a macro view of the end-to-end process and capturing all the relevant information pertaining to material and information flow. The objective is to get a holistic view of the process and ascertain the hidden opportunities for improvement. This should offer the value stream owner a clear perspective on what needs to be done to improve overall process effectiveness. Following are ways by which one can get a 10,000–foot view of an end-to-end process.

Value Stream Mapping

What is value stream mapping? According to the *Lean Lexicon* by Marchwinski and Shook: "Value stream mapping is a simple diagram of every step involved in the material and information flows needed to bring a product from order to delivery" (Marchwinski and Shook 2003). Don't be concerned with the manufacturing overtones in this definition. The tool is as effective in service companies as it is in manufacturing organizations. It is a simple visual tool that clearly reveals the wastes hiding in processes and the opportunities to be pursued for improving them.

To learn about value stream mapping I recommend the book *Learning to See* by Mike Rother and John Shook. This book provides an authentic approach to value stream mapping in a manufacturing company. However, if you are keen on seeing its application in an office setup, my recommendation would be the book *Lean Administration I* by Bodo Wiegand and Philip Franck.

Figure 2.24 shows the list of icons that are commonly used for value stream mapping. The icons have been adapted from the works of Wiegand and Franck.

The *process box* is quite a powerful icon that allows the capture of all the information that you may require and find relevant. Figure 2.25 shows a number of items that are commonly captured during a service-sector value stream mapping exercise. You can add more information icons as required.

Figure 2.26 shows an example of a value stream map from a financial services company. It will give you an idea as to what it takes to construct a value stream map and its power to reveal wastes and opportunities for improvement.

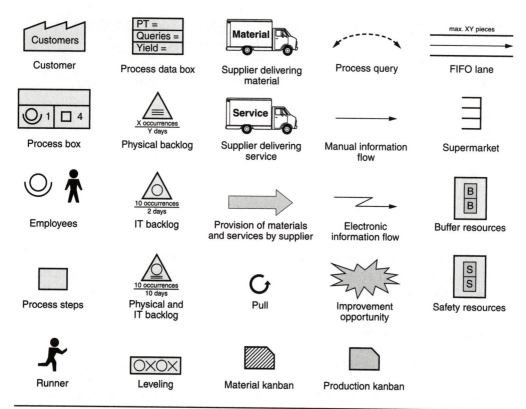

Figure 2.24 Icons used for value stream mapping.

Adapted from: Bodo Wiegand and Philip Franck, *Lean Administration I* (Aachen, Germany: Lean Management Institute, 2006).

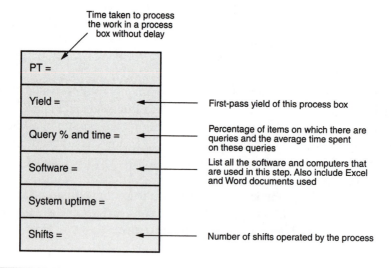

Figure 2.25 The process box yields a plethora of information.

Did You Know?

It is important that you understand the icons clearly before commencing value stream mapping

It is imperative that all participating improvement team members understand all the icons of value stream mapping. This is to avoid confusion. I have seen individuals goofing up on value stream maps because they do not understand lean concepts such as kanban, supermarket, FIFO lane, and so on. Before drawing value stream maps, please ensure that the concepts of lean are understood clearly.

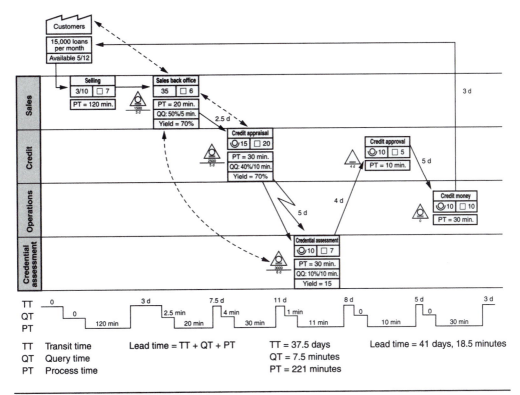

Figure 2.26   Current-state value stream map from a financial services company.

You can make your own icons for value stream mapping

As you master the art of value stream mapping you can make up your own icons. However, whatever icons you decide to use, ensure that the same ones are used across the company. This is required for uniformity and ensuring that all the employees understand what is being communicated.

Value stream mapping can be done using software

Value stream mapping can be done using software, but it is recommended that in the early phases of LMS it is drawn manually. This is to ensure that the individuals who are involved in value stream mapping get a complete understanding of how it has to be done. It is true that manual value stream mapping may be a bit cumbersome, but it is a worthwhile experience as it not only gives a hands-on feel to the process but also builds a camaraderie among the team members carrying out the improvements. The trials and tribulations of value stream mapping bring the team closer together and strengthen the resolve of the team members to solve the problem.

Advantages of Value Stream Mapping

The advantages of value stream mapping are as follows:

- Unseen wastes are revealed
- Depicts both the material flow and information flow in the process
- Clearly brings out opportunities for improvement in end-to-end processes
- Entire process becomes visual before everyone and is available for discussions
- Helps to brainstorm and arrive at a consensus on the future state desired in a process
- Tells you where you can remove time from the process
- Determines the cycle time versus actual value-added time in a process
- Can be used as a strategic planning, change management, and communication tool

Baseline the Existing Value Stream Map

The outcomes of value stream mapping include not just the existing as-is map but also a list of process data points that can trigger actions. The data points comprise performance indicators and other information that impact the final outcome of the process. While the performance measurements are captured to gauge the health of the existing process, the other information points provide data on how they impact performance outcomes. The endeavor should be to capture a set of metrics that give a holistic view of the performance of the process. Many of these data points can be captured during the value stream mapping exercise while some may need to be gathered after the mapping exercise.

So, what are the data points that should be captured and listed as a part of this exercise? The following is a list of the key data points:

- *First-pass yield.* This is the percentage of the product that leaves the process without defects and without having to be reworked. This is a powerful metric for measuring the effectiveness of processes.

  Traditionally, organizations have calculated yields at the end of the process by looking at the good product produced. These good products also included items that may have been reworked during processing. An example calculation is depicted in Figure 2.27.

  Out of the 100 units that entered the process (see Figure 2.27), there were 20 units that were defective after the first process step. In the second step, out of 80 units input, 15 are defective. However, after step 1, of the 20 defectives produced, 10 are reworked. Similarly, after the second step, out of the 15 defectives, five are reworked.

  Traditionally, *yield* (also called *final yield*) has been calculated by looking at the outputs produced at the end of the process and includes defective items that have been reworked.

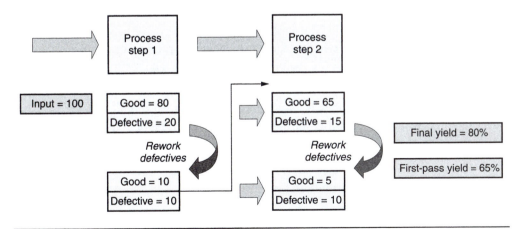

Figure 2.27 Example of first-pass yield calculation.

It is okay to capture the yields of some of the in-process steps

During value stream mapping, the yields at intermittent process steps should also be captured. It may not always be possible to capture the yield at every process step. But even if you get the yields of some of the process steps, it will be very helpful.

So, following the above methodology,

$$\text{Yield} = \frac{80 \times 100}{100} = 80\%$$

There is another yield statistic that every professional should be able to calculate: first-pass yield. This is the number of units made minus the defectives that have been reworked. This gives a true picture of your process. Hence:

$$\text{First-pass yield} = \frac{65 \times 100}{100} = 65\%$$

It is imperative that whenever you calculate yield, do not just look at final yield but also find out the first-pass yield. This will help you to reveal the hidden factories or non-value-added activities in your process. All your projects should endeavor to improve the first-pass yield of processes.

- *Productivity levels.* This is the measurement of the rate of a process, an efficiency measure to ascertain how fast processing gets done. Examples of productivity measures include transactions processed per hour, calls handled per hour, transactions per teller, number of sales per FTE (full-time equivalent).

- *Customer satisfaction.* This is a measure used to determine the effectiveness of a process. It establishes whether the attributes of the product or service provided meet the requirements of the recipient of the process. The recipient could be the next person in the process or the end user of the product or service.

- *Customer complaints.* This is another data point that we should look for. Essentially it means looking for the number and the type of complaints that are being reported.

- *Demand.* This refers to the rate at which the customer desires a product or service from an organization.

The following are the various times that should be a part of the baseline:

- *Takt time.* This is a measure of the pace of customer demand.

Did You Know?

The word *takt* has German origins

The word *takt* is taken from the German, which means *rhythm of music*. Takt time determines how fast a process needs to run to meet customer demand. It is about having a rate of processing that meets the rate of sales. The endeavor should be to make the entire process be driven by the takt time. Here's how it is calculated:

$$\text{Takt time} = \frac{\text{Net available working time per day}}{\text{Customer demand per day}}$$

"Net available working time per day" is total work time minus meetings, breaks, lunch, and other non-value-added activities.

Takt time is expressed in time units, such as "one every so many minutes."

Example of takt time calculation

In a financial services company, there is a demand for 500 credit cards per day. What is the takt time of the process? (Assume that the cards are processed in one shift every day and the duration of a shift is eight hours, of which 30 minutes is devoted to breaks, lunch, and meetings.)

$$\text{Takt time} = \frac{(8 - \frac{1}{2}) \times 60 \times 60 \text{ secs}}{500} = \frac{27,000}{500} = 54 \text{ seconds}$$

This means one card needs to be processed every 54 seconds to meet the current customer demand.

In the case of the processing happening over two shifts in a day, the takt time would undergo the following change:

$$\text{Takt time} = \frac{(8 - \frac{1}{2}) \times 2 \times 60 \times 60 \text{ secs}}{500} = \frac{54,000}{500} = 108 \text{ seconds}$$

So if the organization runs two shifts, one card needs to be processed every 108 seconds.

Lessons to Ponder . . .

The pace of a process should be modified based on takt time, which reveals the pace of customer demand.

- *Pitch.* Pitch is a multiple of takt time and is the rate at which work units can be flowed through a process. It is adopted when items can't be flowed at the rate of takt time and is often seen in high-volume transactional environments. In such a case, if the items are not moved per the pitch, a large number of runners will be required.

- *Lead time.* This is the end-to-end time required for execution of a process, which starts at the time the customer places the order and ends when the customer receives the product or service. This was explained in detail in Chapter 1.

- *Throughput time.* This is the time taken to complete a process. This was also explained in Chapter 1.

- *Process time.* This is the time taken to complete the activities of a process without any delay.

- *Query time.* This is the time spent addressing the queries in a process. It is quite common in service and transactional processes and is a symptom of a process bottleneck.

- *Waiting time.* This is the time that the items in the process wait to be worked on. Waiting time in a value stream map is calculated by days of inventory of materials, physical documents, and information.

- *Travel time.* This is the time spent moving items, material, documents, and information.

- *Transit time.* This is calculated by adding *waiting* and *travel* time in the value stream map.

- *Cycle time.* This is the time taken to complete the smallest work unit (also called a *task*). It is the time taken by an associate to complete one task before it can be repeated again. Cycle time could include a large number of work elements.

- *Hassle time.* This is the time spent by consumers interacting with the organization for not getting the product or service right the first time. Hassle time is the result of inefficient processes because of which the organization may need to deal with the customer more than once. Hassle time is something that organizations should be measuring if they are concerned with bettering the customer experience.

- *Process efficiency.* Also called *value-added ratio,* this is the ratio of time spent on doing value-added activities to the total lead time of the process. This was explained in detail in Chapter 1.

Did You Know?

Pitch is a compromise

Yes, pitch is a compromise when items can't be flowed per the takt time of a process. For example, in a credit card back office wherein large number of applications get processed in a day, it may not be practical to move applications per the takt time. This is when the concept of *pitch* is adopted:

$$\text{Pitch} = \text{Takt time} \times \text{Number of work units*}$$

(*Number of work units that need to be grouped to move at the desired pitch.)

Let's assume that, on average, 5500 credit card application forms get processed in a day (assume one-shift processing) and the duration of the shift is eight hours, which includes 30 minutes of breaks, lunch, and meetings.

$$\text{Takt time} = \frac{\text{Net available working time per day}}{\text{Customer demand per day}}$$

$$= \frac{(8 - \frac{1}{2}) \times 60 \times 60 \text{ secs}}{5500} = 4.9 = 5 \text{ seconds}$$

This means that every five seconds one application form needs to be processed and moved to the next workstation. However, this may not be practically possible. So, as a compromise, pitch is adopted.

Let us assume that we decide to move the application forms every half hour. So this is the pitch, and we need to find out the number of work units that need to be grouped to move at this pace.

$$\text{Pitch} = \text{Takt time} \times \text{Number of work units}$$

$$30 \times 60 \text{ secs} = 4.9 \times \text{Number of work units}$$

$$\text{Number of work units} = 367$$

This means that to maintain a pitch of 30 minutes, application forms need to be moved in bundles of 367 (see Figure 2.28).

If you believe that the bundle size is too large, try and reduce the pitch. However, you will then require a larger number of runners.

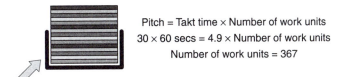

Pitch = Takt time × Number of work units
30 × 60 secs = 4.9 × Number of work units
Number of work units = 367

Figure 2.28   Representation of a bundle corresponding to a pitch.

Take average demand for calculating takt time

To calculate takt time for a process, consider the average demand for the last six months. If you believe that the demand changes much more aggresively, you can use average demand for the last three months. This is often the case for products and services whose volumes are increasing in leaps and bounds, for example, in emerging markets such as India and China.

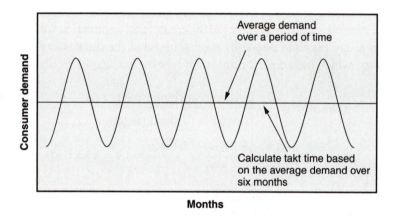

Figure 2.29 Using average demand to calculate takt time.

All of the above data points are required for baselining the process before you can actually commence improvement. In service organizations it is sometimes possible that all of these data sets may not be captured. In such cases, a mechanism first needs to be installed to capture these metrics. While manual data collection may not be the ideal thing to do, sometimes you may have to go ahead and capture data manually just to begin work on a project.

While doing the initial baselining it is possible that data collection may not be perfect. Don't worry. Even if the readings are a bit imperfect they will be sufficient to begin work.

The View from Five Feet

Having decided on the desired future state of your process, the next thing is to carry out improvements in areas that have problems. This is where detailed process analysis should be done. This will be discussed in step 14.

If the takt time has a large amount of variability, design-in a two-standard-deviation cushion

If demand is highly variable, it causes major variation in takt times. To avoid this it is recommended that you design-in a gap of two standard deviations between the associate cycle times and the takt time. This is depicted in Figure 2.30. A 2σ cushion will ensure that there is 97.5% chance of takt time being more than or equal to cycle time. (This is obtained by 95% area of the normal distribution covering 2σ on both sides of the average takt time $(\bar{x})$ + 2.5% of the area lying beyond 2σ on the top.) Of course, there will be a 2.5% chance of takt time being less than the cycle times or existing work distribution not being adequate to meet the customer requirements.

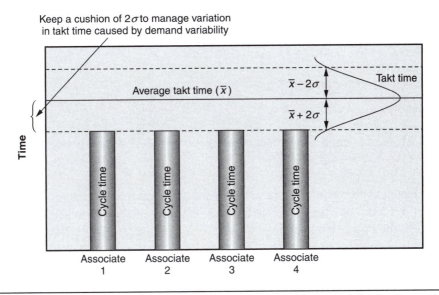

Figure 2.30 Cushion of two standard deviations for high variability in demand.

STEP 13: VISUALIZE THE FUTURE STATE

Having completed the as-is value stream mapping, the improvement team sits together to decide the future course of action. The entire team, comprising the value stream owner, process owner, lean navigators, LMS manager, IT specialist, lean maven, and process associates, meets in a room to discuss and understand the value stream map and how to improve it to take performance to the next level. Getting together this team, representing the entire value stream, not only gets buy-in but also helps to tie improvements to

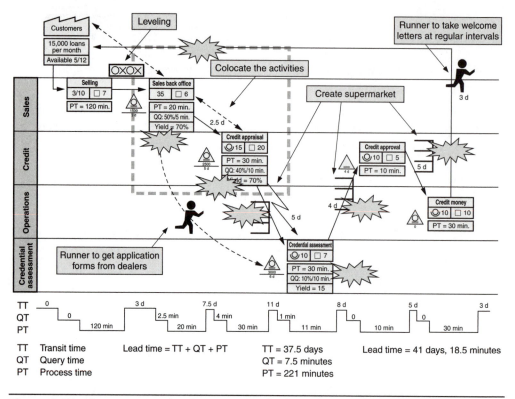

Figure 2.31 Future-state value stream map of a financial services process.

strategic business objectives. The future-state meeting happens in a meeting room (often called "war room" or "future room") where the current-state map has been drawn. Figure 2.31 shows a partial future-state map of a process in a mortgage finance business. While developing the future-state map, apply all the relevant principles of lean such as flow, pull, takt time, supermarket, and kanban. Clearly mark on the future-state value stream map the areas wherein lean breakthroughs/improvements need to be carried out.

Brainstorming the future state is quite an intense exercise on which leaders may be required to spend as much as two days. I can tell you personally that it is well worth it, as the quality of the value stream map that is created will determine the performance expected of the organization. Sometimes it is decided that the implementation will happen in a phased manner, so in addition to the current state and future state, the interim state and aspirational state are also determined. Remember, the aspirational state value stream map should strive to meet the long-term vision of your organization. The aspirational state could be achieving objectives such as "being the best customer service company in the world." Between the future state and aspirational state, there could be many interim states (see Figure 2.32).

One of the outputs of the future-state brainstorming session is to arrive at an action plan to implement the interim and future states. The template used for this is shown

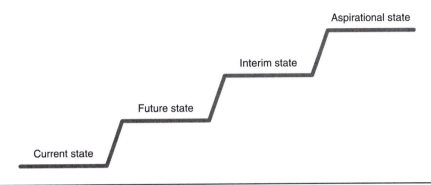

Figure 2.32   Phased future-state implementation.

							Review dates		
Process number	Process owner	Implementation accountability (who)	Lean maven (who)	Teams	Interim state (when)	Future state (when)	J	F	M

Date: _____

Name of the value stream: _____ Value stream owner: _____

Ver: 1

Exhibit 2.3   Template for master list of processes to be improved for future state.

in Exhibit 2.3. As can be seen, the template acts as a master list for the value stream owner to know which processes are being worked on and who has taken accountability for them.

This template is backed with a detailed implementation plan (Exhibit 2.4) for each of the processes.

Having listed the areas that require improvement, you can decide on the type of methodology to be used. It is recommended that you adopt the right approach based on the complexion of the problem. Table 2.9 summarizes the different types of problems and the corresponding approaches to be used.

One of the commonly used approaches to deploying improvements is the lean breakthrough. This is discussed in detail in Chapter 4.

It should be noted that steps 14 and 15 pertain to the actual implementation of improvements.

	Date: _____
Name of the process: _____	Process owner: _____
Lean maven: _____	

| What* | Who | | When (completion dates) | | | | | | Review dates |
	Accountability	Team	Jan	Mar	May	Jul	Sep	Nov	

*List all the improvements/projects that will be done to achieve future state.   Ver: 1

Exhibit 2.4 Template for detailed implementation plan for future state.

Table 2.9 Problem types and methodologies to be adopted.

Type of problem	Quality approach to be used
Variation	Six Sigma, statistical process control
Lack of processes	Install standard processes
Waste	Lean tools and techniques
Low yields	Seven QC tools, QC story, Six Sigma
Lead time/delivery	Lean tools and techniques

Lessons to Ponder . . .

Select improvement approaches based on the context and type of problem. A one-size-fits-all approach does not work; one methodology can not be used for all improvements.

STEP 14: DISSECT PROCESS AND CARRY OUT DETAILED PROCESS ANALYSIS

Value stream mapping was about looking at a process from 10,000 feet. And this step is about looking at processes from five feet. In this step, we zoom in on the areas where improvements are required (this is shown in VSM by the icon of "improvement opportunity"). This step dissects the process in detail and reveals the wastes.

Commence this step with a *process walk*. This is about physically following the materials and information flow to get to know what exactly is happening in the process and revealing the hidden wastes.

A process walk is a science as well as an art; there are a lot of things that need to be accomplished. The following are the items that need to be accomplished during a process walk:

- Identification of both seen and unseen wastes

- See how the process actually is executed

- Understand how problems are identified

- Triggers for problem identification

- Hear the comments that are exchanged between the process associates

- Identify steps taken to correct problems

- Identify errors that may be committed in the process and steps taken to correct them

- Ascertain how team leaders react to problems

- Determine the type of metrics and how they are tracked in the process

- Determine whether work processes are standardized

- Identify the level of mistake-proofing in the process

- Determine how technology contributes to the execution of the processes

Cycle Time of All Work Units

The process walk should be accompanied by a *time observation* study. The objective of this exercise is to capture the time taken to complete the smallest unit of work. It includes the time it takes an associate to complete one task comprising several work elements before they are repeated. This can be captured using the time observation sheet template shown in Exhibit 2.5. This exercise should be done meticulously. Do not just take one reading for each of the activities, but go for at least 15 readings.

The time observation study helps you to determine the cycle time of the process steps/activities. It should be done meticulously to ensure that the correct readings are captured; use a stopwatch.

Detailed Value-Added versus Non-Value-Added Analysis

While doing the process walk, capture and segregate all the activities in detail and list the actions that need to be taken on them.

Exhibit 2.6 can be used to list and segregate the types of wastes in the process. All the process steps are listed and segregated into value-added, non-value-added, or business-value-added.

Process step	Cycle time															Reading to be considered
	Readings															
	1	2	3	4	5	6	7	8	9	10	11	12	13	14	15	

Date: _____

Consider the second-best repeated readings.   Ver: 1

Exhibit 2.5 Template for time observation sheet.

Date: _____

Type of waste	Process activities*						
Value-added							
Non-value-added							
Business-value-added							

* All the activities in process steps have to be listed in the empty boxes.
Use the symbol "✓" for segregating the activities.   Ver: 1

Exhibit 2.6 Segregation of value-added steps from others in a process.

Ascertain Time Consumption of Activities in Process Steps

In an organization commencing a lean transformation, the primary focus should be on the following times:

- *Wait time.* This is the time spent in the process when the item or work unit is waiting to be worked on.

- *Travel time.* This is the time spent in the process when the item or work unit is traveling between workstations, floors, and locations.

- *Rework time.* This is the time spent in the process when the item or work unit is being reworked.

The template shown in Exhibit 2.7 is used to find out the time consumption for each of the process steps.

The author has seen from experience that most of the improvement projects taken up in services pertain to problems with wait and travel times. Eliminating them helps to remove many of the wastes hiding in service processes.

Lessons to Ponder . . .

- Given the large number of "times" that are used in lean, it is a must that you understand them before really trying to make use of them for improvement

- The captured cycle times of work units could contain a large number of wastes that have to be eliminated as a part of lean improvements.

Date: _____

Process step	Value-added/ non-value- added/busines- value-added	Cycle times*			Total cycle time (A + B + C)	Other times				Total time
		Value- added time (A)	Non- value- added time (B)	Business- value- added time (C)		Wait time (D)	Travel time (E)	Any other time 1 (F)	Any other time 2 (G)	
	Total times									
Total throughput time = A + B + C + D + E + F + G										

* Cycle time refers to the time an operator takes to complete a task before it is repeated.   Ver: 1

Exhibit 2.7 Template for determining activity times for each of the process steps.

Spaghetti Diagram

This is a tool used to ascertain the work flow of items of a process that is being analyzed. It helps to establish the layout of the process by finding out the distance traveled by material, items, documents, or people. It reveals the large distances traveled and inefficient layouts existing in the process. After looking at the spaghetti diagram, the endeavor should be to reduce the distances traveled in the process.

The visual nature of the spaghetti diagram reveals about the process that which we normally do not get to know. Remember, the larger the distance traveled in a process, the less efficient it is. The spaghetti diagram opens up a dialogue between all stakeholders of the process on how it can be improved. Don't forget to measure the distance traveled before and after the improvements.

Exhibit 2.8 is a template for making a spaghetti diagram of a process.

Lessons to Ponder . . .

The spaghetti diagram helps to demystify the geography of processes and reveals opportunities to reduce the distances traveled.

STEP 15: DEPLOY LEAN SOLUTIONS

Having identified the wastes, the team should brainstorm lean solutions for the desired future state of the process. This can be quite tricky in a service organization as the typical solutions that are implemented in a manufacturing company may not be applicable. What is required is that they be applied intelligently using the basic principles of lean. Some of the key techniques that are applied in service companies are explained below. All of these tools and techniques endeavor to create *continuous flow* and *pull* in processes.

Let us understand these two concepts throroughly and the associated techniques that help in achieving them.

Continuous Flow

This is about sequencing activities so that they move in a flawless manner. The objective here is to ensure that an item that is being worked on does not get held up in the process. In continuous flow, the processing of items happens in time with the demand from the customer. Processing happens when needed—no more, no less. In case there is less work, the system balances itself to ensure that every individual working on the process has equal work.

A common procedure in many processes, Figure 2.33 shows an example of batch and queue processing in a mortgage business. As you can see, the files pile up on the

Date: _____

Spaghetti diagram

Business unit:

Value stream name/no:

Process name/ID:

Process selected for spaghetti analysis:

Start point: _____ End point: _____

Process owner:

Date: _____

Number of associates: _____

Number of workstations: _____

Number of process steps: _____

Broad process flow

Ver: 1

Exhibit 2.8 Template for spaghetti diagram.

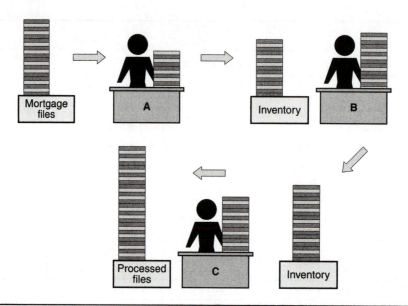

Figure 2.33   Batch and queue flow in mortgage processing.

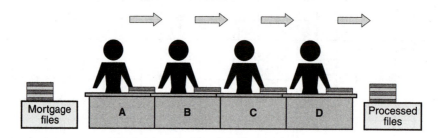

Figure 2.34   Continuous flow in mortgage processing.

tables of processors as well as in between workstations. This is quite common in service companies that have not been touched by lean.

Figure 2.34 show how the process flow comprised of isolated islands has been converted into continuous flow. Note how inventory levels have been reduced substantially. The ideal scenario, and the principle that drives processing in continuous flow, is to process one item at a time.

Application of continuous flow leads to the following benefits:

- Major reduction in lead times

- Drastic reduction in work-in-process inventory levels

- Processing happening per customer demand

- Proper load distribution among process associates

- Process adjusts to flexible customer demand

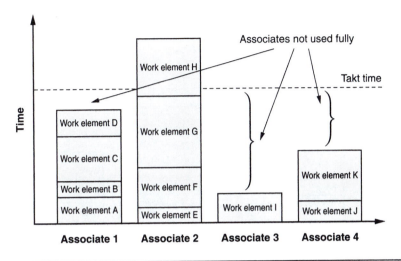

Figure 2.35 An example of an associate balancing chart.

- Faster detection of problems
- Less hassle and fatigue

Line Balancing

This is a mechanism to evenly distribute work among the associates in a process with the objective of meeting takt time. This tool optimizes the utilization of personnel so that all associates are doing more or less the same work content. To achieve this, the *associate balancing chart* (shown in Figure 2.35) is quite handy.

Associate Balancing Chart. This is a graphical display of the work done by each process associate in comparison to the takt time.

Required Number of Associates. The number of associates required in a process can be derived using the following formula:

$$\text{Number of associates} = \frac{\text{(Total cycle time)}}{\text{Takt time}}$$

Let's look at an example (see Figure 2.36). There is a data entry process that has four associates working on it. Currently the work content is not balanced among them. The associate balancing chart shows work content distribution in terms of cycle times. As is shown, the cycle time of work done by each associate includes various work elements that take different times.

Total cycle time of a process = Sum of the individual cycle times

Total cycle time of this process = Cycle time of associate A +
Cycle time of associate B + Cycle time of associate C + Cycle time of associate D

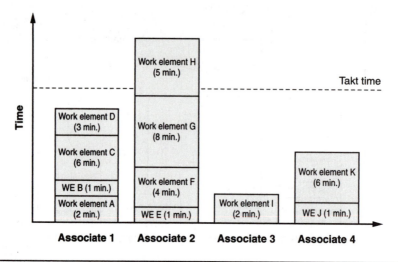

Figure 2.36   Work content of associates in a data entry process.

Total cycle time of this process = 12 mins + 18 mins + 2 mins + 7 mins = 39 mins

$$\text{Number of associates that should be in the process} = \frac{(\text{Total cycle time})}{\text{Takt time}} = \frac{39}{15}$$
$$= 2.6 \text{ people}$$

There is a clear opportunity for balancing the load between associates in the process and also redeploying at least one person.

The approach that should be adopted to accomplish this is as follows:

- Try and eliminate the non-value-added work elements of each of the associates, especially associate 2 and associate 1

- Merge work elements wherever possible, especially the work elements of associate 3 and associate 4, and associate 1 and associate 2

This is shown in detail in the associate balancing chart, Figure 2.37.

Buffer and Safety Resources

The focus of all lean process improvements should be to remove any bottlenecks and ensure that processes run in a flawless manner. However, this may not always be possible for the following reasons:

- Despite improvements, all the process bottlenecks may not be removed at once but has to be done in a phased manner

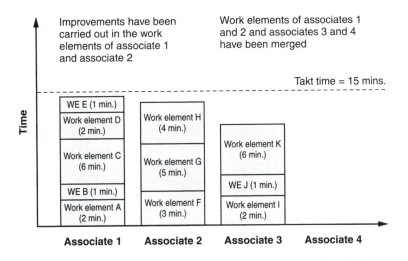

Figure 2.37   Associate balancing chart after improvements.

In case your manpower numbers are in decimals, do not round them off to the next highest figure

Often, after calculating the associate numbers in a process, the results are in decimals. Table 2.10 shows the approach that should be adopted.

Table 2.10   Action plan for associate numbers in decimals.

Number	Associate number decimals	Action to be taken
1	.1–.3	Remove non-value-added work elements and reduce cycle times. Do not add extra people.
2	.4–.5	Remove non-value-added work elements, see if work elements can be transferred to another associate. Do not add extra people.
3	.6–.7	Remove non-value-added work elements, transfer work elements to another associate, and run the task for ten days. See if the cycle times come down. If not, add one person.
4	.8–1	Remove non-value-added work elements; you are free to add one associate to the process.

- While improvements may have been carried out, it is taking some time to bring stability to the process

- Customer demand varies erratically

Under such circumstances, as a compromise, *buffer resources* and *safety resources* are used. Table 2.11 differentiates buffer and safety resources.

Buffer and safety resources are similar in nature and should be backed with a solid exigency plan. Without such a plan, their implementation may not be easy.

Typical buffer and safety resources are as follows:

- Overtime

- Holiday pay

- Temps

- Flexible manpower

- Retired personnel

- Multi-skilled employees

Figure 2.38 shows how a process should be treated in case there are sudden spikes in demand. Use buffer resources in such instances. However, please note that using buffer resources requires that they be trained fully and there is a well-laid plan for dealing with demand spikes.

Lessons to Ponder . . .

Remember, safety and buffer resources are only stop-gap arrangements in your process transformations.

Table 2.11   Difference between buffer resources and safety resources.

Buffer resource	Safety resource
This is a cushion in the process to take care of varying customer demand	This is a cushion in the process to take care of inefficiencies in the process
Buffer resources should be used to manage sudden spikes in demand	Safety resources could be required because of process bottlenecks, lack of training, equipment issues, or mismatch of capacities

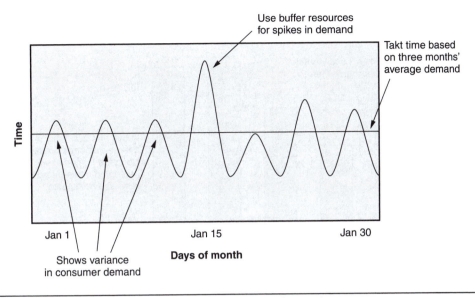

Figure 2.38 Buffer resources for sudden spikes in demand.

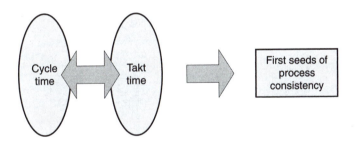

Figure 2.39 The confluence of cycle time and takt time.

Cycle Time and Takt Time Relationship

Understanding the relationship between cycle time and takt time is critical in lean process improvement. While cycle time represents the voice of the process, takt time represents the voice of the customer (demand). Effectively managing cycle time and takt time is the first step to process consistency and reliability (see Figure 2.39).

One of the first things that should be accomplished is to balance the cycle times. We have seen a bit of this under "work content balancing." So what happens when the work contents of process associates vary as reflected in cycle times that are not balanced? This situation has been captured in Figure 2.40. Dissimilar cycle times cause in-process inventory accumulation and result in products and services not being delivered on time to the customer or even being defective.

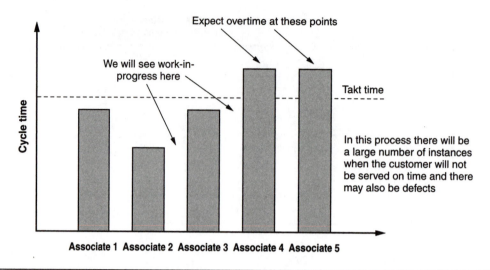

Figure 2.40 Impact of varying cycle times in a process.

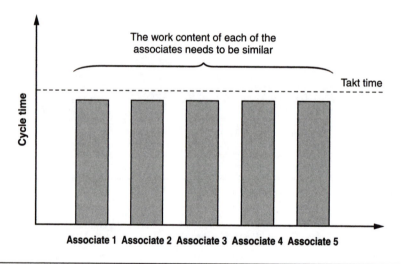

Figure 2.41 Associate work content balancing chart.

Following are the steps to be followed to create an optimum relationship between cycle time and takt time:

1. Begin by balancing the work content of the associates, leading to them having similar cycle times. This is achieved by removing the non-value-added work elements in the work content of the associates and merging work elements among the associates. Having improved the cycle times, the associate work content balancing chart will look as shown in Figure 2.41.

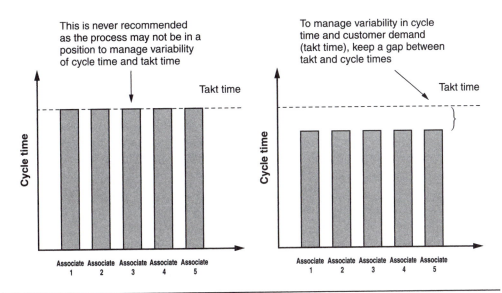

Figure 2.42 Gap between cycle time and takt time.

2. The cycle time should not match with the takt time. There has to be some gap between cycle time and takt time. This is required in order to manage the variations of cycle time and takt time. While cycle time variability can be reduced through training, takt time can not be controlled by the organization since it is driven by the customer (see Figure 2.42).

5S

Before commencing with installing standard processes, it is imperative that you apply the principles of 5S. This is a simple yet extremely powerful methodology that facilitates workplace organization.

It has five simple steps, which are as follows:

1. Sorting

2. Systematic arrangement

3. Spic 'n' span

4. Standardization

5. Self-discipline

For details on approaches to 5S implementation, I recommended that you refer to the author's book *5S for Service Organizations and Offices: A Lean Look at Improvements,* published by ASQ Quality Press.

Lessons to Ponder . . .

Don't undermine 5S by looking at it as a housekeeping tool. It is an approach that has direct impact on all processes operating in a workplace.

Standard Process

Constancy of cycle times in processes can be achieved by ensuring that associates follow the same process every time. This is not easy and requires *standard processes*.

What is a standard process? It is the best known method of doing the work. It is based on industry benchmarks, current process capability, technology requirements, and future state of the process, and is put down in a written form so that everyone can understand. The objectives are customer convenience, ease of execution by the employees, consistency, and making the job easier.

For details on processes, procedures, and performance standards please refer to Chapter 1.

It needs to be mentioned that consistency of work can also be achieved through optimized work content and desired skills:

$$\text{Consistent work} = \text{Optimized work content} + \text{Desired skills}$$

Optimizing Work Content

Optimization of work entails ensuring that the non-value-added work elements of a process are eliminated and value-added content improved. To ascertain the time spent on the work elements it is recommended that you use the *standard work combination table* (Exhibit 2.9).

According to *Lean Lexicon* by Marchwinski and Shook: "A standard work combination table shows the combination of manual work time, walk time, and machine processing time for each operator in a production sequence." (Marchwinski and Shook 2003)

The standard work combination table helps us to determine the work elements that comprise a task or work unit. It essentially summarizes the work elements that make up the work unit of an associate. The standard work combination table has to be made up for each work unit. Each of them has to be broken into elements and their respective times captured while segregating them as waiting, walking, manual, and electronic. Compare the cycle times with the takt time of the process. It should be your endeavor to reduce the cycle time by removing the non-value-added work elements and reduce the time of value-added elements by making them more efficient. The standard work combination table provides a brilliant approach to dissecting cycle times and revealing wastes that are often taken for granted in service companies.

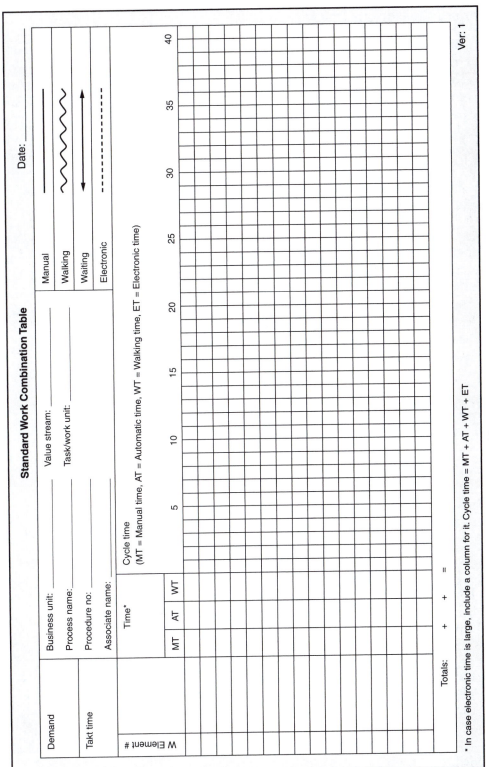

Standard Work Combination Table

Date: _____

Demand		Business unit: _____	Value stream: _____
Takt time		Process name: _____	Task/work unit: _____
		Procedure no: _____	
		Associate name: _____	

Manual ———————
Walking ∿∿∿∿∿
Waiting ↕
Electronic - - - - -

Cycle time
(MT = Manual time, AT = Automatic time, WT = Walking time, ET = Electronic time)

W Element #	Time*			5	10	15	20	25	30	35	40
	MT	AT	WT								

Totals: ___ + ___ + ___ + ___ =

Ver: 1

* In case electronic time is large, include a column for it. Cycle time = MT + AT + WT + ET

Exhibit 2.9 Template for standard work combination table.

Standard Operations Display

This is a chart that is often overlooked and underestimated in service companies; people do not realize its power. It is used to give an overview of the sequence followed by process steps in a workplace. The chart clearly tells the associates how the operations happen and the contribution of his or her work. The *standard operations display* should be a one-page document and should be visible to all relevant people in the process. The standard operations display shows details such as standard work-in-progress, inspection points, and how work gets accomplished. A template for a standard operations display is shown in Exhibit 2.10.

Layout

The objectives of layout modification during lean transformation of a process are to create independent, optimized, all-encompassing operating units that use minimum space with all activities sequentially placed next to each other, usually processing for a specific product family. This allows items to be processed in a continuous flow or in small batches. The most common cellular layouts are the U-shape (Figure 2.43) and straight line (Figure 2.44).

The following are a few principles that need to be kept in mind when designing cellular layouts in service organizations:

Date: _____
Standard Operations Display
Number: _____   Release date: _____

Business unit:	
Value stream name/number:	Process owner:
Name of the process:	Number of associates in this operation:
Process no./ID:	Average demand:
Start point: _____ End point: _____	Takt time:
Number of procedures:	
Procedure numbers/IDs:	
Operation details (How are the steps in the operation sequenced? Mention the cycle time of each task)	Visual representation of the operation (Draw the diagram showing the sequence of operations and illustrating the manner in which the operations move)
Signature of team leader:	Signature of process owner:
	Ver: 1

Exhibit 2.10   Template for standard operations display.

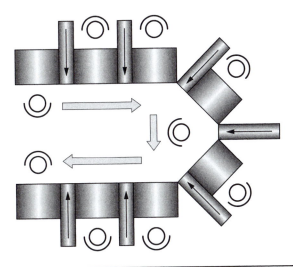

Figure 2.43 U-shaped cellular layout.

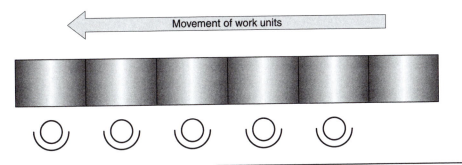

Figure 2.44 Example of straight-line layout.

- Arrange workstations close to each other and keep minimal gaps between them to ensure that inventory does not pile up

- Ensure that the cell is staffed with individuals who have all the required skills to execute the process and facilitate ongoing corrections

- Avoid creating specialization; focus on multi-skilling of all process associates

- Reduce batch size to the minimum

- Keep all the workstations and table tops at the same height

- Empower cells to take their own decisions; let the process not wait for approval from outside the cell

- To take care of peaks and valleys in demand, utilize the multi-skilled staff to fill in where needed

- Eliminate reentry of data

- Use work procedures, check sheets, and visual management to ensure standardization and mistake-proofing

- Design the cell to handle the major process flows; to handle exceptions use another cell.

Multi-Skilling of Employees

Multi-skilling of employees is at the heart of lean improvement. Efficiency in a workplace increases dramatically when individuals are able to perform varied jobs. This is not easy and it is recommended that a senior leader in the organization take ownership of multi-skilling of employees. Without top management commitment and repeated reinforcement, multi-skilling can never be attained. This is especially challenging in service companies in emerging economies such as India, Vietnam, and China wherein the attrition of employees is very high. More information about multi-skilling can be found in Chapter 1.

Multi-skilling of employees can't be achieved overnight. In the early phases of lean implementation we should focus on the practice of "+1 to –1." This is essentially about ensuring that a process associate becomes familiar at least with the skills of the preceding and succeeding steps in the process.

Lessons to Ponder . . .

Multi-skilling of employees is a must for service companies wishing to survive in today's competitive environment.

Did You Know?

Multi-skilling is not multitasking

Do not confuse multi-skilling and multitasking.

Multi-skilling is about an individual being equipped with varied skills that will allow him or her to be used for multiple jobs in a workplace. The person takes up another task only when the current work in hand has been completed.

Multitasking is about an individual doing more than one task at a time. This should be avoided at all cost. Here the person gets into another task before completing the first task. This does not increase efficiency but instead produces wastes of incomplete and defective work.

Pull

This is a mechanism for managing the flow of resources in a process by replacing what has been consumed. It is about providing what is needed, when it is needed, on time, every time, in the stipulated quantity. In a pull system, production is triggered by a signal based on what has been consumed, unlike a push system wherein production is based on historical sales trends or forecasts or "to store/to inventory." Under a pull system we create a mechanism wherein the upstream process produces only when the downstream process gives a signal. The objective that drives pull is to avoid producing more than required. Do not make anything other than what the customer wants.

The concept of pull can be summarized by four words: "use one, make one."

One of the tacit objectives of pull is to stop operations in case there are any abnormalities due to quality issues, equipment breakdown, and so on. So, when the line stops, the organization will be forced to get to the root cause of the problem immediately.

Lessons to Ponder . . .

Remember, having made the process flow, the endeavor should be to instill a regimen wherein production happens at the pull of the customer.

While single-piece continuous flow should be the objective of all lean process improvements, it may not always be possible. This is when we accept a compromise such as a *FIFO lane and supermarket* (Figure 2.45). In these cases we design-in inventory between process steps and still ensure that the process is able to meet customer requirements. This will be discussed in detail later in this chapter.

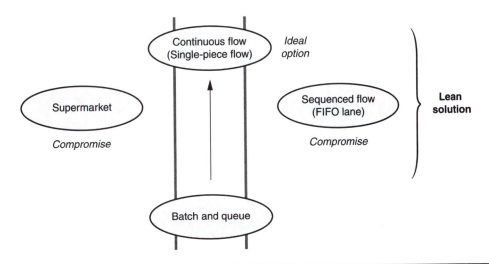

Figure 2.45   The FIFO lane and supermarket approach to lean solutions.

Little's law: The little-known but powerful law

Enunciated by John. C. Little, a professor at MIT Sloan School of Management credited for his seminal work in operations research methodology, traffic signal control, decision support systems, and especially marketing, one of whose pioneering works in operations research is known as Little's law.

Little's law states that the average number of works-in-progress in a stable system is equal to the completion rate multiplied by their average time in the system. This relationship is shown as:

Work-in-progress = Throughput time × Average completion rate

The above relationship can also be shown as follows:

Throughput time = Work-in-progress/completion rate
= Work-in-progress/Input rate = Work-in-progress/Output rate

To understand this better, let us look at a mortgage loan office (see Figure 2.46) wherein the mortgage application forms enter and exit at a constant rate of 100 files per day. If the average inventory of application forms at any given moment is 800 forms, we can use Little's law to find out the throughput time, or the average time that the files are in the shop. Using Little's law, the throughput time will be eight days.

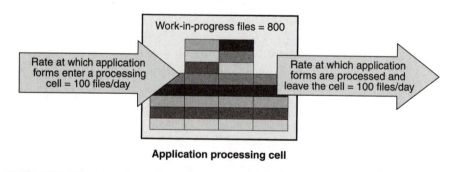

Application processing cell

Figure 2.46   Mortgage loan office example showing entry and exit of application forms.

Little's Law and Lean

Little's law helps to explain a principle that drives lean projects.

As we know, a goal of all lean projects is to reduce throughput time of processes. This can be done in two ways. We can either increase the completion rate or reduce the amount of work-in-progress (WIP).

The completion rate can be improved by investment in capacity, equipment, and technology, or addition of people. When implementing lean, this approach should never be adopted until all available low-cost possibilities have been exhausted. Given this, the option remaining is to reduce work-in-progress. This is exactly what we try to do in lean projects wherein the primary focus is on WIP reduction (see Figure 2.47).

Little's Law in Customer-Facing Workplaces

It should be noted that when the WIP in a process is people, the principles shown in Figure 2.48 should be applied. Examples of such workplaces are retail bank branches, airline ticketing stations, subway ticketing stations, quick-service restaurants, and so on.

For example, for a bank teller, when the number of customers in the queue goes up and the required standard throughput times need to be maintained, the focus should be to improve the completion rate. This can be achieved by adding capacity to the process by opening a new teller counter. This is generally what is done intuitively even without knowing or applying Little's law.

Little's Law and Pull

Little's law can come in very handy to create pull with processing cells. To create pull, the objective of a cell should be to maintain a stipulated WIP (also called *calculated threshold*) that has been arrived at based on the desired standard lead time and the

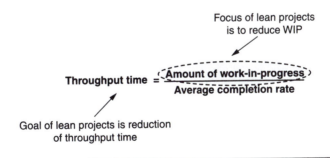

Figure 2.47   Little's law and lean projects.

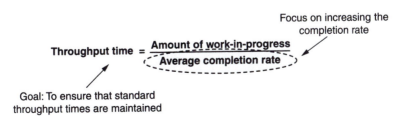

Figure 2.48   Little's law in customer-facing locations.

processing (completion) rate. The endeavor should be to maintain the calculated WIP and restrict entry of items until the WIP in the cell is reduced below the calculated threshold. To explain this point, let us look at an auto finance credit processing cell.

The following are some of the process data:

The average rate at which the application forms get processed = 100 per day (that is, on average, 100 files get processed each day by this cell)

The standard throughput time within which the application forms need to get processed = 12 hours (.5 days).

Let us use Little's law to find out the desired WIP to ensure that the throughput time of 12 hours (.5 days) is maintained. We incorporate the data into the formula for Little's law, which is as follows:

$$.5 \text{ days} = \frac{\text{Desired work in progress}}{100 \text{ application forms/day}}$$

Desired work in progress in the cell = 50 application forms

This means that in order to meet the throughput time of .5 days, at any given moment in time the average WIP in the cell should be 50 application forms. The team should put in place a mechanism to ensure that additional application forms do not enter the cell until the number of WIP in the cell falls to 49.

This can be achieved by using an electronic signal as shown in Figure 2.49. The cell pulls in inventory only when the inventory falls to 49, at which time a runner replenishes the inventory from a supermarket.

FIFO Lane

A FIFO lane is a mechanism used to regulate work flow wherein a defined quantity of inventory is held between two workstations. The inventory items are loaded sequentially and are held between the supplying process step and the consuming process step. The upstream process stops production when the lane is full.

The FIFO lane can be visualized as a tube between two processes that holds inventory. The supplier process stops producing when the tube gets full and does so until the consuming process almost completely liquidates the inventory. Only when most of the inventory is consumed does the supplier process commence production again (see Figure 2.50). Remember, the smaller the FIFO lane, the lesser the inventory and throughput time. The size of the FIFO lane is determined by the capacity of supply, customer demand, consuming processes, and process constraints that may not yet be resolved.

FIFO lanes are typically used for the following types of items:

- Customized inventory

- One-of-a-kind products

- Products with shorter shelf life

- Expensive inventory items required infrequently

FIFO lanes are used when it may not be practical to keep inventory in a supermarket.

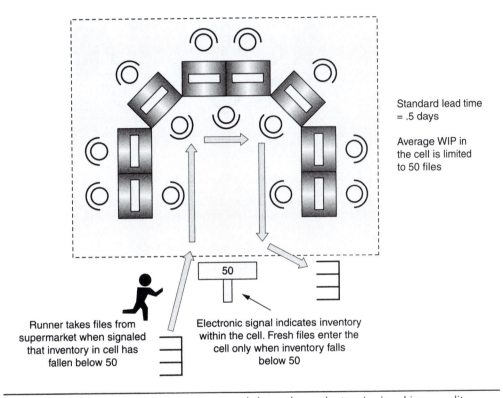

Figure 2.49   Stipulated inventory managed through an electronic signal in a credit processing cell.

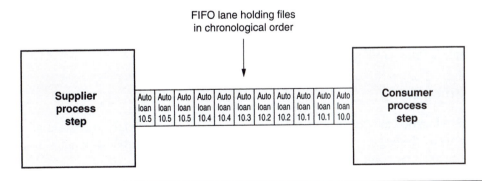

Figure 2.50   FIFO lane for documents between two process steps.

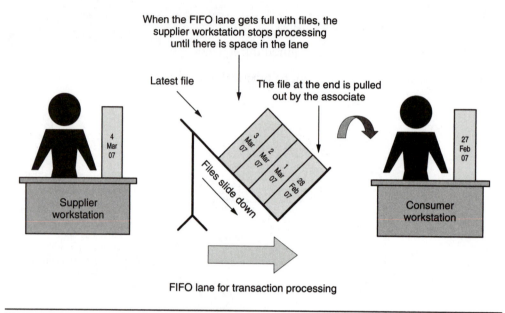

When the FIFO lane gets full with files, the
supplier workstation stops processing
until there is space in the lane

Latest file

The file at the end is pulled
out by the associate

FIFO lane for transaction processing

Figure 2.51   Example of an innovative FIFO lane in transaction processing.

Figure 2.52   Example of a file holder that can be used as a FIFO lane.

In services, it pays to be creative when designing a FIFO lane. Figure 2.51 shows an innovative FIFO lane designed for a transaction process unit.

A simple file holder can also serve as a FIFO lane between two workstations. An example is shown in Figure 2.52.

Supermarket

This is a location to store inventory (work-in-progress or completely processed) that can be pulled by the customer and later replenished by the supplier process. It helps in scheduling an upstream process that will flow continuously.

This lean technique is based on the storage principles of the supermarket that all of us visit for our daily wares. Supermarkets are repositories of tightly managed inventories that facilitate pull in processes. A supermarket does not hold much in inventory, and

Did You Know?

Why the supermarket icon used in value stream mapping opens toward the left

The supermarket icon (Figure 2.53) used in value stream mapping is open on the left as this side belongs to the supplier process.

Figure 2.53   Supermarket icon.

items are replenished directly from the manufacturing unit or a distribution center as soon as they are picked by the customer from the shelves. The supermarket does not have costly storage space and sources, just the quantity of items that can be placed on the shelf for consumption.

In lean, a supermarket is used to schedule an upstream process. Remember, it is a compromise like "pitch and buffer" and is done only when one-piece flow is not possible.

Before implementing a supermarket, ensure that continuous flow has been achieved in as many processes as possible. Typically, supermarkets should be near the point of use and should be loaded from the back. They are then pulled from the front by the customer process. This ensures minimum WIP in the customer process.

Typically, supermarkets are used under the following conditions:

- Processes are designed to operate at a faster pace or in a closer space

- Processes are located at a distance from each other

- Processes cannot be colocated

For more information about supermarket and pull, I recommend the book *Creating Level Pull: A Lean Production System Improvement Guide for Production Control, Operations, and Engineering Professionals* by Art Smalley. Though it talks about supermarket application in manufacturing it can be easily adapted for service companies.

Lessons to Ponder . . .

Do not try to eliminate all of the inventory in processes until the upstream processes that make and hold your inventory have been addressed.

Kanban

Kanban in Japanese means *signboard*. It is a visual management tool used to manage and regulate the flow of work units. It can be used in a supermarket, storage area, rack, and so on. Kanban is a tool that facilitates inventory management. All information that helps in inventory movement is included on a *kanban* such as what, when, how many, who, and so on.

In service processes, both physical and electronic kanbans are used. However, whatever the type of kanban used, they perform two functions in service processes. They signal an upstream process to make a certain item; this is called *production kanban*. They also authorize the movement of items into the downstream process; this is called *withdrawal kanban*. The objective of a supermarket is to provide processing instructions to the upstream process when both the upstream and downstream processes can't be linked in a continuous flow. Remember, the supermarket belongs to the upstream (supplying) process and should be located near it. The onus is on the customer process to get to the supplier supermarket and pick what it needs.

Lessons to Ponder . . .

1. It took 10 years to establish *kanban* at Toyota Motor Company.

2. *Kanbans* allow minimal inventory by improving processes to deliver to customers just in time.

Types of Kanban

In service companies there are generally three types of kanbans used:

1. *Ocular kanbans.* These are kanbans that make use of our eyes. Simple yet highly innovative, these are signals that tell us when an item has to be replenished. Following are some examples of ocular kanbans:

    a. A ribbon on the wall or workstation to indicate when an item needs to be replenished

    b. Kanban boards wherein instead of moving cards in a workplace we move magnets on a board.

    c. Kanban squares

    Kanban squares are quite an effective mechanism to regulate flow between workstations. They are simple squares painted on workstations that hold a certain number of items for processing. When the kanban square in the customer workstation is empty, it is an indication for the process associate

Kanban squares can be very effectively used in service processes

Kanbans need not always be cards. They can be as simple as a square or a rectangle in the workplace or workstation. When the square is empty it is a signal to replenish the item. Kanban squares can be quite useful in service processes wherein papers, files, or dockets move from one workstation to another.

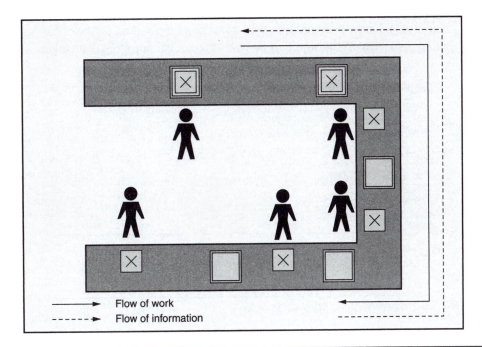

Flow of work
Flow of information

Figure 2.54 Depiction of use of kanban squares.

to commence production. Typically the quantity of items held in the kanban square is just one or two. The use of kanban squares is depicted in Figure 2. 54.

2. *Signal kanbans.* These kanbans are those that trigger the upstream process step to produce when the inventory reaches a minimum threshold in a downstream process step. The signal is triggered when the inventory reaches a reorder point.

3. *Process kanbans.* These are physical cards, which comprise the following types:

a. *Withdrawal kanban.* These kanbans are used to specify the quantity and type of product that needs to be withdrawn from the preceding process step. This could be the supermarket of the preceding process step. An example of withdrawal kanban is shown in Figure 2.55.

b. *Production kanban.* These kanbans stipulate the type and quantity of items that need to be processed by the supplying process step.

c. *Supplier kanban.* These are kanbans that are used to withdraw items from an external supplier.

Figure 2.56 explains how production and withdrawal *kanbans* function in a supermarket. As the items (such as files, documents, materials, and so on) are withdrawn by the customer process from the supermarket, a production kanban or signal is sent to the supplier process to replenish what has been taken.

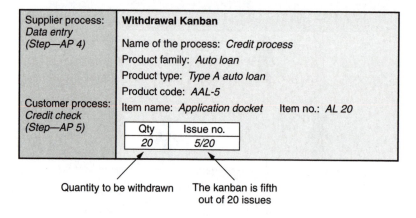

Figure 2.55 Example of withdrawal kanban.

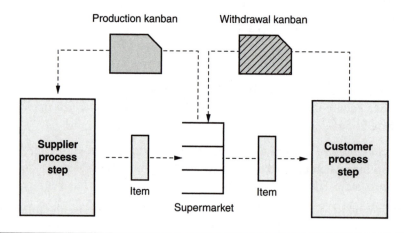

Figure 2.56 Mechanism of a supermarket with production and withdrawal kanbans.

5. *Electronic kanbans.* These are electronic signals used as a kanban. They are typically used between process steps located at a distance or in two different work sites. They help to eliminate the wastes associated with a paper system and facilitate implementing pull in technology-laden service processes. The advantages of electronic kanbans are as follows:

- Helps to get rid of the problem of lost cards

- Reduces the travel time associated with sending the kanban

- Problems associated with faxing kanbans are eliminated as there are no illegible faxes

- Enhances communication in the entire process

- Provides flexibility and facilitates rapid customer response

- Drastically reduces in-process inventory levels

- Instantly provides information to processing points

Examples of electronic kanbans are as follows:

a. Bar codes used in supermarkets to signal consumption when passing the cash register

b. Bard codes used to track movement of files and items

c. Software triggers used to replenish stationery inventory in a bank branch

d. Electronic triggers sent by ATM machines when cash falls below a certain level

e. RFID (radio frequency identification) tag system used for tracking inventory across the value stream and products consumed

Supermarket Size

The quantity of inventory that should be in the supermarket has to be carefully determined so that excess inventory does not get stored.

The inventory level at the supermarket is dependent on the following factors:

- Distance of the supermarket from the supplying process

- Reliability of the process; are there equipment failures?

- Performance of the supplying process (first-pass yield)

- Time spent on changeover (moving from one software program to another, printer setup time)

- Variation in demand by the customer process

Table 2.12 Approach to calculating inventory at supermarkets (finished goods/work-in-progress).

	Average daily demand × lead time to replenish the item (days)	Cycle stock
+	Demand variation* as percent of cycle stock	Buffer stock
+	Safety factor as percent of cycle stock and buffer stock	Safety stock
=		Inventory of finished goods or WIP in supermarket

(*Keep at least two standard deviations of demand as buffer)

The approach to be followed for inventory calculations is shown in Table 2.12.

This method has been taken from the book *Creating Level Pull: A Lean Production System Improvement Guide for Production Control, Operations, and Engineering Professionals* by Art Smalley. The formula is used to establish the quantity that should be stored in the supermarket.

Please note that (a) cycle stock is calculated based on average demand and lead time to replenish the item, (b) buffer stock is the quantity required to cover for customer-induced variation, (c) safety stock is required to cover for quality defects and process downtimes.

Reorder Point

For signal kanbans, there is a need to calculate the reorder point, which can be done by using the simple formula

$$\text{Reorder point} = \text{Cycle stock} + \text{Safety stock} = D \times LT + SS$$

where

D = Demand

LT = Time to replenish the inventory from the time order is placed until it is received

SS = Safety stock

Construction of a Pull System: Integration of Supermarket, Kanban, and FIFO Lane

Instituting a pull system in a service process is dependent on the type of process, customer needs, and context. Following are the typical options applied to service companies:

1. *Build to order.* In this construct all products and services are manufactured to demand (Figure 2.57). No finished-goods inventory is stored and products are manufactured after an order is received. Such processes, when looked at end-to-end, have relatively low inventory but require stable processes that have short lead times. Examples of such a system include:

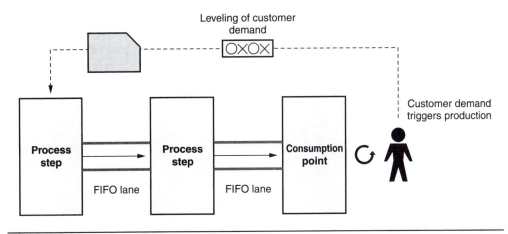

Figure 2.57   Build-to-order pull system.

    a. A customer placing an order for a demand draft in a bank branch

    b. Customers walking into a fine-dining restaurant and placing an order for food

    c. Customers placing orders with a financial organization for products such as home loans, auto loans, and so on

Lessons to Ponder . . .

A build-to-order system requires a high level of process capability and the ability to deliver to customers on short notice.

2. *Build to store.* In this case, some inventory of finished product is stored so that customer demand is met on short notice. However, it should be noted that the inventory should be minimal to ensure that excessive storage space is not required. In this construct, production commences after the consumption of stored finished product (see Figure 2.58). Examples of build-to-store systems include:

    a. Finished pizzas, burgers, and so on, are stored in display cabinets at airports, malls, and so on, so that they can be quickly microwaved and given to the customer on demand

    b. An inventory of ATM cards is kept in bank branches so that they can be given instantly to a customer who walks in to open an account (yes, this ATM card may not have the name of the customer embossed on it, but he or she can use it immediately after generating their PIN at the branch)

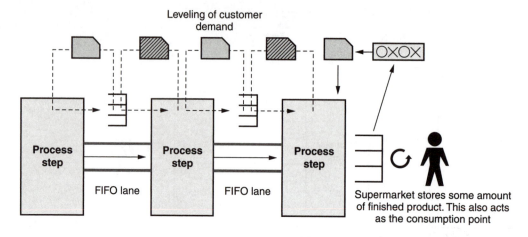

Figure 2.58 Build-to-store pull system.

Leveling

Customer demand varies in all service processes. There can be days when the demand for products or services is higher than on other days. Varying customer demand is a reality and organizations should be in a position to manage it. This is where the technique of *leveling* is used.

Leveling is a mechanism for distributing the work required to meet customer demand over a period of time. The objective is to align customer demand with the pace of the process while still being able take care of oscillating customer demand.

A process may need to be leveled to manage either varying volume or varying varieties and types of products.

A lean process works in a stable manner and is running at a set pace. However, if the pace of the process keeps changing, sometimes the work balance and standard work will be disrupted. To avoid this, we use the technique of leveling, which is about managing customer demand so that the process continues to operate at the defined pace in an efficient manner despite demand oscillations.

Heijunka Box or Leveling Box

A tool commonly used to level processes is the *heijunka box*. As per the *Lean Lexicon*, a heijunka box is a tool used to level the mix and volume of production by distributing kanban within a facility at given intervals. (Marchwinski and Shook 2003.)

Figure 2.59 shows a heijunka box wherein the vertical column on the side represents the product types and the horizontal row on top shows time. The slots represent the material and information flow timing while the kanbans in the slots show the pitch of production of one of the product types.

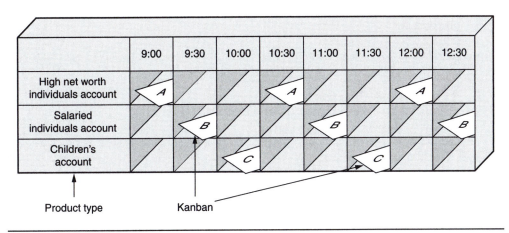

Figure 2.59 Example of a heijunka box.

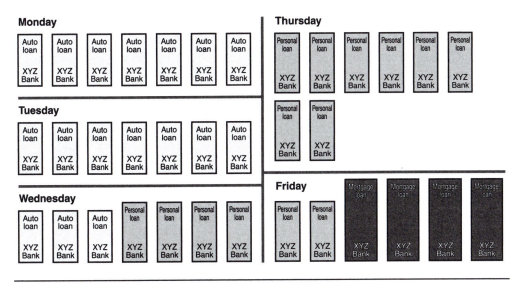

Figure 2.60 Unleveled processing of financial products—daily schedule.

Figure 2.60 shows an example of a financial services back office wherein an asset manufacturing line does the processing of auto loans, personal loans, and mortgage loans. Since the demand for auto loans is very large, they get processed on Monday, Tuesday, and part of Wednesday. The personal loans, which are second largest in demand, get processed on Wednesday (partially), Thursday, and part of Friday. As the demand for mortgage loans is less, they get processed only on Friday.

This results in the following:

1. Increased lead times for processing

2. Pile of inventory

Figure 2.61 depicts leveled processing wherein all three types of products get processed every day. This is called *mixed model leveled production.*

Creative Ways to Level Consumer Demand

Beyond the heijunka box, service companies are finding creative ways to level consumer demand, such as:

- "Happy hours" in a restaurant

- Patients given specific times for doctor appointments

- Specific programs to woo customers during non-peak hours

- Cheaper air tickets during the time period of 11 AM to 3 PM when flights are not availed by business travelers

- Special gifts to customers in a mall during lean/non-peak times

- Incentives to customers to use the call center during non-peak times by giving extra loyalty points to credit card customers

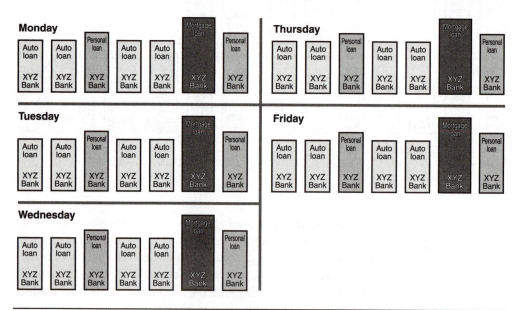

Figure 2.61 Leveled processing of financial products—daily schedule.

Principle behind the bullwhip effect

Based on the work of J. Forrester, the *bullwhip effect* is a phenomenon observed in forecast-driven processes wherein customer demand magnifies as one moves up the supply chain (see Figure 2.62). To manage variability in customer demand, organizations forecast to meet customer requirements.

However, forecasts are often not correct, so inventory buffers are built across the process. Moving up the process from downstream to upstream, the stakeholders (departmental functions) observe greater variation in demand and hence the need for more safety stock. This phenomenon may be triggered by varying order quantities, frequency of orders, or a combination of both. The results of the bullwhip effect are excess inventory, inept customer service, and excessive customer service.

The answer to the bullwhip effect is to move away from a forecast-driven process to a demand-driven process.

The bullwhip effect is also called the *whiplash effect*.

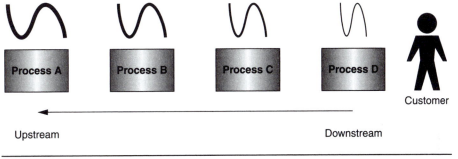

Figure 2.62   The bullwhip effect.

Lessons to Ponder . . .

The bullwhip effect increases process costs substantially.

The objective of this book is to provide insight into some of the solutions that can be applied in service organizations. Solutions have to be customized based on the specific problem and context.

Did You Know?

The *runner–repeater–stranger* framework can be used for scheduling service production

The runner–repeater–stranger framework emanated from Lucas Industries in the late 1980s and can be quite handy in segmenting product families that have to be produced. Products are divided into three groups based on customer demand:

1. *Runners* are typically products or product families that have high demand and less variability in product types. These are to be manufactured as and when required. Volumes are sufficient to have a dedicated line or cell.

2. *Repeaters* are those that have medium customer demand and product (type) variability. The production of these items has to be scheduled on a regular basis but a dedicated line or cell may not be warranted.

3. *Strangers* are products and product families that have low demand and high variability. These are low in priority and are typically scheduled around the repeaters.

This concept can be very effectively used in services. It helps to greatly enhance efficiency, especially in a high-volume transactional context wherein processing is scheduled after doing a Pareto analysis and scheduling is based on the runner–repeater–stranger framework.

ASSIMILATE	Decide	Decide on measurements and dashboards
	Implement	Implement and instutionalize the processes

STEP 16: DECIDE ON MEASUREMENTS AND DASHBOARDS

Having implemented lean solutions, your organization should decide on what measurements to take. The metrics chosen should reflect the following:

- *Voice of the process.* These are metrics that capture the nominal process performance.

- *Voice of the customer.* These are the outcome metrics of the customer's view of the process performance.

- *Voice of the business.* These are metrics that capture the overall performance of the business or value stream.

- *Voice of the employees.* These are metrics that measure the engagement of the employees in the implementation of the lean management system.

- *Voice of LMS implementation.* This is a holistic measurement of the health of the lean management system in an organization.

Lagging versus Leading Indicators

It has been seen that organizations often install lagging measures without really worrying about leading measures. This is not very effective. A company should have a balance of both leading and lagging indicators in their processes. So what are leading and lagging indicators?

- Leading indicators are metrics that are tracked while the process is being executed. They typically help to predict the outcome of the process.

- Lagging indicators are metrics that are measured after the process has been executed. They are critical for an organization but taken too late to correct problems. They measure the result/outcomes of a process.

Lessons on Measurements

The following is a list of lessons that have been learned by the author during lean management system implementations. It is imperative that these are kept in mind while deciding on and commencing with measurements:

1. Take an integrated view of measurements; look for metrics that cut across functional silos and give an end-to-end perspective.

2. Use a common language on the metrics that are being measured so that everybody in the organization understands it. You cannot afford to have two definitions of a metric in an organization.

3. Have well-defined measurement protocols so that the operational definitions for the measurements are clear to all concerned in the organization.

4. Create mechanisms for automatic collection and capture of data through digitization at relevant places.

5. Measurements should be strategically aligned to the performance scorecard of the business.

6. Define clear ownership for all metrics.

7. Create organizationwide buy-in for the metrics that are installed in the process loops.

8. Metrics need to be action-oriented.

9. The CEO and top leadership should be provided with a dashboard that shows performance of all the process loops in the value streams.

10. Review of lean metrics to be a key item on the agenda of top management.

11. All metrics should have a clear drill-down path whereby the user can move from a higher level to a lower level and vice versa. The information should be digitized and virtually real-time.

12. Have a regimen of reexamining the metrics every 12 months; the relevance of metrics changes over time.

13. Install leading and lagging indicators. Lagging indicators could be output or outcome metrics.

14. Avoid manual collection of data, as it may not be sustainable over time. The endeavor should be to digitize data collection.

15. Management should be worried if they never hear about bad news in processes; do not create a culture wherein employees are rebuked for sharing information about poor process performance.

16. The organization should have a single holistic digitized dashboard for the CEO and other top management. This would contain multiple summed-up metrics across value streams. These can then be "drilled down" to various levels for relevant hierarchies in the company.

17. When commencing with measurements, ensure that they are implemented within six to eight months (possibly more for a large multi-locational organization). This is required to "shock" the organization to quickly adopt a metrics-driven performance culture.

18. In the workplace, make the measurements visible so that employees know how they are performing. Let the measurements not hide in computers. Display them either on whiteboards or even digital dashboards

19. Clearly stipulate responsibility for all data collection, data storage, and data security (see Exhibit 2.11).

20. Go beyond process metrics; also look at metrics that measure organizational and customer engagement and business results. Figure 2.63 summarizes the types of metrics that should be installed as part of LMS implementation.

Details	Data capture	Data storage	Data security	Data disposal
What (What needs to be done?)				
When (When will this need to be done?)				
Who (Who will do it?)				
Where (Where will this be done?)				
How (How will it be done?)				
Why (Why should it be done?)				
Overall ownership				
Review responsibility				

Date: _____

Ver: 1

Exhibit 2.11 Data collection template.

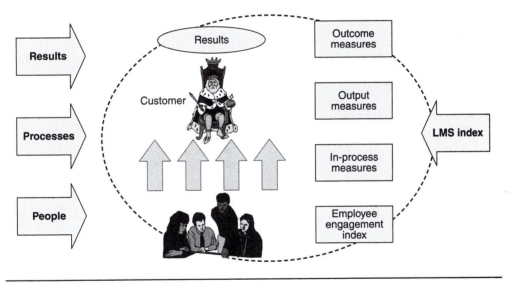

Figure 2.63 Holistic view of metrics.

It is recommended that the organization have a tracking system that provides aggregate and detailed information on performance. Leaders should be in a position to view drill-downs by business, value stream, geography, function, customer, roles, selected time periods, and workplaces. Creating a Web-based dashboard may be very useful as it can provide real-time visibility of performance levels to all employees. When all functions and departments in a value stream get measured, every employee understands how his or her activities contribute to the larger organizational objectives.

STEP 17: IMPLEMENT AND INSTITUTIONALIZE THE PROCESSES

Having decided on the measurements to be taken, the organization should commence with implementation of the new lean processes and the processes that help the lean processes to sustain their gains. The two broad types of processes that need to be implemented are:

- *Improved processes.* These are processes that have been improved using lean techniques.

- *Management processes.* These are the processes that help to support the improved processes and the lean management system. Rollout of these management processes should happen after all the value-creating processes have been rolled out. Some of the typical management processes that are installed as part of LMS implementation are:

  - Root cause analysis

  - Process management architecture

  - Process governance

  - Process change/new process introduction

  - Performance management

  - Change management

  - Corporate governance

Assimilation of the new processes will require everybody in the organization to be trained on the improved processes and the relevant measurements.

SUSTAIN	Audit	Ascertain health of lean management system and processes through assessments and audits
	Improve	Launch ongoing improvement regimens

STEP 18: ASCERTAIN HEALTH OF THE LEAN MANAGEMENT SYSTEM AND PROCESSES THROUGH ASSESSMENTS AND AUDITS

In addition to measurements, which are quite an effective tool for assessing the performance of a lean management system, an organization undergoing a lean transformation also needs to put in place a regimen of audits. The LMS office, who provides assurance to top management on the health of processes and the lean management system, should carry out the audits. Such audits are discussed in detail in Chapter 3.

STEP 19: LAUNCH ONGOING IMPROVEMENT REGIMENS

Launching a regimen of continual improvement is key in a lean transformation journey. Improvements should happen on an ongoing basis and should comprise both large improvement projects and local improvement projects.

Large Improvement Projects

These are improvements that have an impact on the entire organization. They are typically driven by a central team, which could be from the corporate office or a team that has been formed for a specific purpose. Large improvements endeavor to fundamentally modify the way the business is run and must be rolled out across the organization. These improvements deliver radical results and are owned and reviewed at the level of top management. They require a lot of cross-functional participation and buy-in. Successful execution of these projects often requires introducing change management elements. Implementation of such projects requires an elaborate deployment architecture and multi-level ownership. In service organizations, large-project membership includes process owners, lean navigators, lean mavens, LMS managers, information technology specialists, and process paragons. An organization initiates such improvements when it embarks on an LMS implementation. This is done while developing the key processes for improvement.

Local Improvement Projects

These are improvements that are carried out by local teams in a workplace and targeted to solve localized problems. Local improvements not only help in problem solving but help in building a continual improvement culture. Large improvements are initiated, run, and owned by the corporate office. In these cases, the local teams, at most, participate as team members and do not own their end-to-end execution. In contrast, local improvements are initiated, run, and owned by the local workplace.

Local improvements help an organization in the following ways:

- They help to solve problems that are confined to a specific area and do not require an enterprisewide intervention

- They facilitate involvement of the entire organization in the lean transformation

The importance of both large and local improvements is probably best explained by Figure 3.8, page 182. While large improvements raise the overall bar of quality, local improvements prevent backsliding on gains made.

The importance of undertaking both large and small improvement projects is also discussed in the following chapter on anchors.

3
Anchors

A nchors are moorings used to implement, secure, and hold gains on the journey of lean transformation. They comprise individuals, teams, processes, partners, and entities that support implementation and ongoing sustainability. They are the foundations on which a robust lean management system is built. If the tools provide the actions in lean implementation, the anchors create the working foundation. Figure 3.1 visually depicts the position of anchors in the DEB-LOREX management system or LMS implementation.

Anchors are installed to serve the following purposes:

• Hold the lean management system architecture

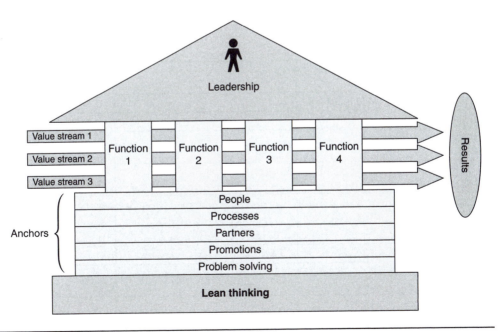

Figure 3.1 The role of anchors in the DEB-LOREX management system.

- Build in-house capability

- Help to sustain the lean management system

I call the anchors the *five P's of the lean management system.* They are detailed in Table 3.1.

Let us look at each of the anchors in detail.

PEOPLE

Most of the roles listed in the category of *people* have been discussed in Chapter 2. Here we will examine the roles that were not discussed.

Table 3.1   Anchors in the five P's of the lean management system.

People	Processes	Partners	Problem solving	Promotions
Value stream owner	Management reviews	Process partners	Large improvement projects	Rewards and recognition
Chief improvement officer	Knowledge repository	Vendors	Small improvement projects	Problem prevention mind-set
Lean maven	Audits		Improvement vault	Brown bag sessions
Process paragon	Performance management			A3 promotion
Process owner	Meetings			Value stream thinking
Lean navigators	Ground zero walks			
LMS managers	Daily meetings			
LMS council				
Dashboard manager				
Chief customer officer				
The customers' cell				
LMS office				
Help desk				
LMS marketing manager				
Human resources department				

Chief Customer Officer

The *chief customer officer* (CCO) is an important individual in an organization's journey to LMS implementation. The CCO owns and represents the customers in the organization. If the organization does not have a CCO, it should create this as a senior-level position reporting directly to the CEO. A *voice of customer* (VOC) cell led by the CCO will gather the impact of the lean processes on the customers. While the chief improvement officer owns and catalyzes all kinds of improvements in the organization, the CCO owns the customers. The CCO puts together a larger service strategy targeted toward differentiating the organization through superior customer experience.

In their endeavor to optimize their processes, functional silos within companies often do a great job in meeting their objectives while forgetting the needs of the end customer. Due to these blind spots within functions, the needs and requirements of customers are often not met. Because of the blind spots within functions, there are service failures that impact overall customer satisfaction. Not having a chief customer officer can lead to customers becoming "orphans" (see Figure 3.2). This leads to proactive steps to understand the needs and wants of customers not being taken, and no one in the company taking ownership to respond to queries from customers. The chief customer officer has the overall responsibility of communicating to all stakeholders the changing needs of customers. Translating customer needs into language that is understood by the process owners is a key role of the CCO. Often customer needs are not met because of the faulty translation of customer needs into process inputs. The chief customer officer also integrates the activities of the various silos and makes sure that the sum of their activities adds up to what the customer requires. The CCO also helps to measure, monitor, and manage customer perceptions and facilitates the building of a "service culture." The CCO also works toward creating a service innovation center to pilot and develop new products that will differentiate the organization from its competitors.

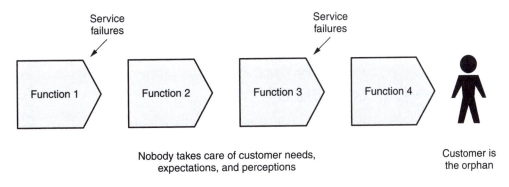

Figure 3.2 Service failures happen when no one "owns" the customer.

Table 3.2   Key focus areas for the chief customer officer.

Problem resolution. Helps to resolve customer pains and problems	*Service measurement.* Measures and monitors the service performance of key customer outcomes	*Service culture.* Catalyzes building a service culture to better customer relationships	*Service training.* Ensures that employees are trained on topics pertaining to services management
Service innovation. Develops and pilots new products that will differentiate the organization	*Experience management.* Works toward bettering the customer engagement and experience with the company	*Service strategy.* Creates a service strategy to differentiate the company through superior customer experience	*Service benchmarks.* Gathers service benchmarks from across the industry.

The following are the roles that are expected of the chief customer officer (see also Table 3.2):

- Understand the needs and requirements of customers
- Build a customer service strategy
- Communicate customer needs and requirements to the key stakeholders
- Translate customer needs into process inputs
- Facilitate selection and administration of tools to gather the voice of the customer
- Ensure that the voice of the customer is captured for the products or services being offered by the organization
- Run programs that aim to improve the customer experience
- Facilitate incorporation of the customer experience into all processes
- Help in installing customer-centric metrics in processes
- Identify opportunities to acquire new customers
- Work out strategies for customer acquisition and retention
- Reveal potential customer defections
- Identify trends in the domain of customer service excellence
- Ensure that all customer queries are handled
- Share key customer metrics with the top leadership and other management
- Regularly pilot service innovations to develop new products that differentiate the organization from the competition

- Improve the process of customer engagement and the service experience

- Gather best practices and service benchmarks from across the industry

The chief customer officer works with the chief improvement officer and LMS office to execute improvements of process failures and performance gaps. As organizations outsource processes, they need to make sure that they do not cede control of the processes to a third party. Even if the processes are outsourced, the chief customer officer should integrate these activities into the larger whole.

Lean Management System Office

This is the corporate cell within the organization that catalyzes the lean management system implementation. The LMS office reports to the chief improvement officer.
The roles to be performed by the LMS office include the following:

- Scripting the organizationwide strategy for LMS implementation in alignment with the top leadership. Ensuring that LMS is an integral part of the larger improvement road map of the organization.

- Assisting value stream and functional leaders in revealing opportunities for improvement.

- Providing thought leadership on matters pertaining to LMS and improvements.

- Ensuring that the LMS effectively develops, manages, and exploits knowledge within the organization and that value streams and functions are able to access this knowledge with ease.

- Helping to create capabilities for LMS implementation within the various functions and value streams.

- Keeping tabs on emerging trends in the domain of improvement and process excellence.

- Providing assurance to the chief executive officer and respective functional leaders and value streams on the health of the processes.

- Facilitating both internal and external benchmarking.

- Houses experts on multiple improvement approaches such as lean, Six Sigma, Lean Six Sigma, and lean process management.

- Advancing the reputation of the organization by showcasing the work done on LMS and improvements.

- Interacting with cutting-edge technology experts and leveraging these resources for improvements.

The Customers' Cell

The *customers' cell* is led by the chief customer officer. The customers' cell is the team that supports the CCO in meeting his or her objectives. The team members in the cell work toward achieving the objectives listed in Table 3.2. The customers' cell also acts as a laboratory to pilot new service innovations targeting differentiation of the organization on service excellence. This team especially focuses on improving the overall customer experience, which comprises both technical and emotional components.

The proposed structure of the customers' cell is shown in Figure 3.3.

Help Desk

The role of the help desk is to support the project teams during their efforts to make processes lean. A help desk is a team within a lean management system set up for ongoing query resolution to problems being faced during implementation. The help desk should put in place multiple channels for gathering questions and queries from lean navigators, LMS managers, and other employees.

The help-desk team should be manned by at least one individual who has the technical competencies to answer the queries. When staffing with a technically competent person is not possible, the help-desk leader should ensure that he or she talks to the

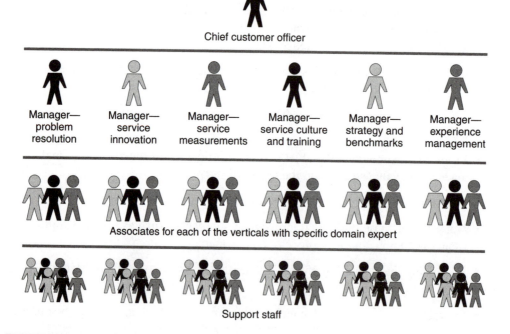

Figure 3.3 The organizational structure of the customers' cell.

experts within the LMS office and gets back to the person who has raised the query within a stipulated time frame.

The following are the channels that organizations install for this purpose:

- *e-mail.* A dedicated e-mail address is put in place to which project and process managers can write for query resolution. The endeavor should be to get back to the sender within 12 to 24 hours.

- *Web site.* There could be a portal where all queries can be posted, with the help-desk team posting the responses on the site. The advantage of this channel is that all queries and responses are visible to all.

- *Help line.* Having a dedicated telephone number is of great help as it allows the query raiser to directly talk to someone about his or her questions. However, it should be noted that a channel like this should necessarily be staffed by a person capable of answering technical queries. Just putting a contact center associate on the job will not be adequate as many of the questions may be technical in nature. However, a help line can be quite effective when an organization is large, with scattered, multiple geographies, and does not have very many experts in lean.

A note of caution on dedicated telephone help lines: all questions should be addressed while the caller is on the line or this channel will lose its sheen.

LMS Marketing Manager

It may sound quite radical to propose the use of a marketing manager for an improvement initiative such as lean transformation!

As we are not selling a product to consumers, it may seem odd that a marketing manager is required. If a CEO is committed and wants to drive LMS, things will happen. This may be true, but it is recommended that a marketing manager be appointed whose objective shall be to sell lean deep and wide in the organization. There may be an opinion that if the CEO mandates LMS, why create another parallel initiative? The way I see it is that mandating alone will cause a few improvement projects to happen, but for LMS to become an integral part of the organizational DNA, it must be moved by the hearts and conviction of people. This will happen when someone sells and continuously communicates the benefits of LMS to the organization.

The LMS marketing manager will sell lean thinking as a product and make sure it is adopted by the employees in the organization. His or her job essentially encompasses selling and institutionalizing lean across the firm.

It may not be easy to find a candidate from outside who has the knowledge of marketing management and also knows the philosophy of LMS. It is thus recommended that a good marketing professional be hired for this role. He or she could be either from within the company or recruited from outside. The primary traits that this individual should possess are a good practicing knowledge of marketing and a solid process orientation. Once on board, he or she should be trained on the basics of the lean management system and the critical success factors required for implementation. The LMS marketing manager reports to the chief improvement officer. The company should expect an individual to function in this role for two years, after which he or she could move into a mainstream marketing function.

The following is a list of the major responsibilities of the LMS marketing manager:

- Establish and communicate the key benefits of LMS deployment

- Create presentation and promotional materials on LMS

- Design various kinds of publicity programs to promote the cause of LMS in the company

- Do personal selling on what LMS is and how it can be a lever for business improvement

- Use telephone, e-mail, Internet, and knowledge management platforms to communicate directly with employees

- Identify influential individuals among the employees (such as the union leader) and take extra time with them on the power of LMS

- Work toward developing word-of-mouth referral channels so that people look forward to getting associated with LMS projects

- Create awareness of LMS among employees through "LMS awareness workshops," which should be made compulsory for each employee

- Share success stories of LMS deployment within and outside the company

An organization can use the following common communication platforms in LMS deployment: brochures, booklets, posters, leaflets, billboards, audiovisual material, videotapes or DVDs, contests, quizzes, exhibits, seminars, publications, events, presentations, and LMS query meetings.

Human Resources Department

Since people are central to LMS deployment, it is a must that the human resources department get involved. Lean is not just about tools and techniques but about building a culture. This is where the human resources (HR) department has to play a stellar role. It has to create a culture that facilitates continual improvement and lean thinking.

The following are a few areas wherein the HR department's partnership is required in an LMS journey:

- *Recruitment and placement.* Hiring from outside or sourcing from within the organization the required talent for LMS implementation such as lean mavens, lean navigators, LMS managers, and so on.

- *Compensation.* Working out a compensation and benefits plan that facilitates recruitment and retention of the best lean talent. Good lean talent is still scarce. Without a thought-out retention strategy, organizations will lose them.

- *Performance management.* Implementing a performance management system that builds a meritocracy within the firm.

- *Best talent.* Ensuring that the best people are seconded to the LMS office and deployed on lean projects. This could be for a period of just two years after which they can return to their parent department.

- *Performance of senior leaders.* Ensuring that business leaders are evaluated on LMS deployment and how effectively they have been able to use it to achieve the organizational objectives.

- *Management trainees.* Ensuring that management trainees and all new recruits are exposed to the basics of lean.

- *Training.* Providing support for nontechnical training programs such as change management, facilitation, and so on.

- *Career progression.* Ensuring that achievements in LMS deployment become a criteria for taking up senior management positions.

- *Leadership alignment.* All existing senior management staff (including the CEO) are made to undergo lean alignment sessions and participate in a lean breakthrough, which means they work on a project as members to feel the rigor for themselves.

- *Employee engagement with lean.* Ascertaining the engagement of employees with lean. This should include regular feedback from employees to hear their "voice."

- *Voice of the employees.* Regularly seek the voice of the employees on the product or service being offered by the company.

- *Culture.* Work with the LMS office to build a culture of continual improvement and lean thinking. Do not forget that the HR department has to be instrumental in facilitating change. This is because institutionalization of LMS is all about change. Change starts with people and it entails the "unfreezing" of old behaviors and "refreezing" of new behaviors. HR has to play a major role, along with the LMS marketing manager, in convincing people as to why LMS should be adopted and how he or she and the company will benefit from it. Unless the individual is willing to change his or her behavior, no change is possible.

Lessons to Ponder . . .

The human resources department should facilitate change that allows lean to penetrate deep and wide within the organization.

PROCESSES

Processes comprise the key anchors that support the lean management system. The key processes follow.

Management Reviews

This process is a key anchor and required for successful lean execution. Despite the best strategies and plans, without adequate management reviews the execution of the lean management system will never happen in an effective manner. The following are the objectives of carrying out the management reviews:

- To ascertain the progress of the lean management implementation
- To ascertain the effectiveness of the lean management system in meeting the organizational objectives
- To look for opportunities for improvement
- To ascertain if customers are satisfied with the product or service
- To ascertain the performance of key metrics

Management reviews need to happen at regular intervals at every stage of implementation. They have to be done by all levels of leadership in the company. A successful management review process requires leaders at all levels to carry out reviews to ascertain progress and performance. However, reviews for the LMS should not be separate from the regular reviews done to ascertain business performance. This sends a message to the employees that LMS implementation is an ongoing program for process improvement and not just an enabler of business improvement. Remember, the lean management system is the means for the organization to achieve its organizational objectives and not just an isolated intervention.

Sometimes management reviews are looked at as a meeting to discuss the lean management system. Unfortunately this is not so. They require serious preparation and planning. The management review primarily consists of two steps:

- Preparing for the meeting by collecting and analyzing data
- Reviewing and discussing the data in the meeting and arriving at a course of action

The frequency of management reviews is determined by the stage of the LMS journey and its effectiveness in meeting the larger business objectives. In the early stages of implementation, reviews should occur more often. However, once the LMS is installed and there is no deterioration, the frequency can be reduced.

It is recommended that a calendar be put in place to track the frequency of reviews (Exhibit 3.1).

It is important that all actions emanating from management reviews be tracked. The action points of the last review should be discussed in the subsequent meeting.

Lessons to Ponder . . .

The ultimate objective of management reviews is to improve the overall capability of the lean management system.

Knowledge Management

Knowledge management is an important anchor that should not be left out during the LMS implementation. Knowledge management is not only about storing learning and experience for posterity, but also about building and growing the existing knowledge of the organization. Knowledge is a strategic asset that needs to be managed in an effective manner for companies that are serious about competition and their competitive advantage. The subject of knowledge management is extremely relevant in emerging economies such as India, where attrition levels are high in many organizations. It has been observed that as individuals move on from organizations they carry with them all of their individual expertise, forcing companies to continually "reinvent the wheel" to replace those capabilities.

It is recommended that a knowledge manager be appointed in the LMS office to take ownership of managing this portfolio. The key roles of the knowledge manager include:

- Develop and implement a strategy for managing knowledge
- Route knowledge to all concerned in the organization
- Foster the flow of knowledge across the organization
- Build expertise in the core competencies of the firm
- Help to bring in knowledge from outside the organization
- Provide thought leadership on specific practices
- Work with teams to solve customer problems
- Collect and codify the knowledge existing in the firm
- Own and maintain the databases of knowledge

Review type	Ownership	Membership	Frequency	Status of implementation																								
				Jan		Feb		Mar		Apr		May		Jun		Jul		Aug		Sep		Oct		Nov		Dec	
				Y	N	Y	N	Y	N	Y	N	Y	N	Y	N	Y	N	Y	N	Y	N	Y	N	Y	N	Y	N

Date: _____

Ver: 1

Exhibit 3.1 Template for tracking reviews.

The knowledge manager is like a crusader who is after an invisible asset called knowledge, which nobody can see and do not like to manage in their day-to-day work life.

For more clarity on the other roles of a knowledge manager, I recommended the works mentioned in the references section.

Audits

Once the processes have been implemented there needs to be a mechanism to ascertain the health of the lean management system. One of the best ways of accomplishing this is through ongoing surveillance audits. The organization needs to put in place a structure that mandates that audits be carried out on a regular basis to provide this assurance to the chief executive officer as well as the heads of functions and value streams. The audit structure could either be an independent entity or can reside in the LMS Office.

Audits of the LMS have the following objectives:

- Ascertain the health of the lean management system

- Provide assurance of a stable LMS to top management, value stream owners, and functional heads

- Identify opportunities for improvement

- Alert leadership to potential risks in processes

- Ensure that gaps identified are closed, and report the status of action closures to the leadership

The audits for lean management are of the following types:

- For assessment of the lean management system

- For the improvement of processes

Lean Management System Assessment

This is an assessment done to ascertain the overall health of the lean management system. It endeavors to look at the status of lean implementation from a holistic perspective and identify specific levers that will deliver sustained results. It is a mechanism to ascertain how the components of the management system perform to achieve the business objectives. This assessment can be done using a checklist (see Appendix A). Companies should use the checklist as a self-examination process to proactively find out the areas that they need to work on to get the desired results. Instead of focusing on all identified gaps, organizations can prioritize on specific areas on which the company should work to deliver maximum improvement.

Before commencing with the assessment process, ensure complete alignment with the leadership team so that they are participants in the process. This requires their being able to understand the elements of the lean management system well and what actions need to be taken when gaps are discovered. LMS assessment has to be carried out by individuals trained on the lean management system. Irrespective of function, anyone trained on LMS can execute these assessments. The assessor should be adept at understanding the relationships between causes and effects.

Process Audits

For processes that have been improved, there is a need to install a regimen of process audits. Very often, process improvements deteriorate over a period of time when proper supervision is not present. Together with metrics, audits give a sense to the organizational leadership and process owners of the status of processes after improvements have been carried out. Process audits should be conducted on a regular basis so that opportunities for improvement are revealed and proactive measures can be carried out. Process audits can also be conducted when there is a need to find out the reasons for a problem happening. Process audits need to be carried out by a team comprising a certified process auditor and domain experts. Unlike LMS assessment, which does not require domain experts, process audits require domain experts who understand the nitty-gritty of the process and how it is executed. To make process audits successful it is imperative that there is immense trust between top management and the employees in the process. Otherwise they will be looked at merely as a compliance issue. And when things are not done with the heart in them, there are bound to be problems.

LMS assessment and process audits can be quite confusing. Table 3.3 summarizes the differences between them to help eliminate any confusion that you may have about them.

Table 3.3 Differences between LMS assessment and process audits.

Attribute	LMS assessment	Process audits
Definition	Evaluation of the functioning of a management system and how effective it is in meeting organizational objectives	Evaluation of a specific process to ascertain how effective it is in delivering the desired outputs and outcomes
Team composition	Team of three to six people who have all been trained on assessment of the lean management system	Team of two to four people comprising a certified process auditor and domain experts
Duration	Can take anywhere from four to 10 days based on the size and type of organization	Takes one to three days
Focus	Improvement and self-examination	Compliance with respect to process adherence and regulatory compliance
Sharing of the report	Needs to be shared with the CEO and top leadership of the organization	Needs to be shared with the process owner. May not be shared with the top leadership of the company

Performance Management

This is one of the key anchors in the lean management system. Installing an effective performance management system is a must to drive the right behaviors. Without a direct link to the bottom line, you will never know if the LMS is delivering value. Kaplan and Norton's *balanced scorecard* provides a suitable approach to translating the vision and strategy of the lean management system into action. A typical scorecard should include the organizational vision and objectives broken down into specifics at the level of value streams and functions. It should integrate all the employees to achieve the larger objectives of the company. The performance measures can't afford to reflect myopic goals, rather the intervention of lean should enhance the performance of the entire organization and its strategic goals. One of the critical factors that will drive the success of the lean management system is having the performance scorecard hard-wired to compensation, incentives, and stock holdings of leaders and employees. Figure 3.4 depicts a portfolio of measures that should be tracked in an organization embarking on a journey of LMS transformation.

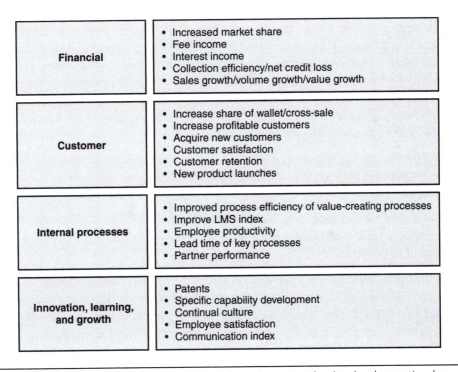

Financial	• Increased market share • Fee income • Interest income • Collection efficiency/net credit loss • Sales growth/volume growth/value growth
Customer	• Increase share of wallet/cross-sale • Increase profitable customers • Acquire new customers • Customer satisfaction • Customer retention • New product launches
Internal processes	• Improved process efficiency of value-creating processes • Improve LMS index • Employee productivity • Lead time of key processes • Partner performance
Innovation, learning, and growth	• Patents • Specific capability development • Continual culture • Employee satisfaction • Communication index

Figure 3.4   Example scorecard of a financial services organization implementing lean management system.

Meetings

Meetings are an integral part of lean transformation. They are required not only during implementation but also during subsequent maintenance of the system. Given this need, it is a must that the meeting process is not only effective but should also deliver value. Large amounts of money are often wasted due to ineffectively managed meetings caused by poor planning, too many or too few participants, poor communication techniques, and so on. Meetings that seem to go on forever and accomplish little or nothing leave us feeling extremely frustrated. So what makes meetings effective? The following are a few guidelines that will make meetings effective and help them to accomplish their intended goal:

- *Avoid a meeting if the same information could be covered in a memo, e-mail, or brief report.* Determine whether the meeting is really required and is the best way to handle the situation.

- *Define the purpose of the meeting and set objectives beforehand.* The benefits of setting objectives for the meeting are twofold: (1) the more concrete your meeting objectives, the more focused the agenda will be, and (2) having specific objectives for each meeting gives you a concrete measure against which you can evaluate the meeting.

- *Develop an agenda in cooperation with key participants.* Before the meeting starts, provide all participants with the agenda, which should include a description of the meeting objectives, a list of the topics to be covered, and a list of who will address each topic and for how long. When sending the agenda you should include the time, date, and location of the meeting and any background information participants will need to know to hold an informed discussion on the meeting topic.

- *Schedule time for preparing for the meeting.* Give participants time to prepare for the meeting. Meeting without preparation may lead you nowhere.

- *Set a time for the meeting to begin and a time for it to end, and then be certain to adhere to these times.* This will allow the participants to plan the rest of their workday.

- *If possible, arrange the room so that members face each other, that is, in a circle or semicircle.* For large groups, try U-shaped rows. Choose a location suitable to your group's size. Small rooms with too many people get stuffy and create tension. A larger room is more comfortable and encourages individual expression.

- *Encourage group discussion to get all points of view and ideas.* Keep conversation focused on the topic. Feel free to ask for only constructive and nonrepetitive comments. Tactfully end discussions when they are getting nowhere or becoming destructive or unproductive.

- *Zero in on actions.* Don't finish any discussion in the meeting without deciding how to act on it. Listen for key comments that flag potential action items and don't let them pass without addressing them during the meeting.

- *Summarize agreements reached and end the meeting on a unifying or positive note.*

- *Evaluate the meeting.* Assign the last few minutes to allowing every person to answer the following questions: What worked well in this meeting? What can we do to improve our next meeting?

Following these guidelines will make your meetings much more effective and you will see the results for yourself. As lean transformation gets under way, master the art of conducting meetings. It is recommended that all key members of the company be trained on how to run meetings and put in place a mechanism to constantly monitor their effectiveness.

Ground Zero Walks

An important facet of lean transformation is that leaders have their "ears to the ground" to find out what is happening in the workplace. Instead of confining themselves to their air-conditioned offices and depending on others for information, they should find out for themselves what's happening in the workplace. The actual workplace or office is called "ground zero." They are so called because that is where the action happens. It is imperative that top management stays connected with the happenings in the workplace. Business leaders, managers, and office supervisors should leave their offices and go to the place where lean implementation is happening or has happened. They should understand the pulse of the workplace and should listen to what people are saying. They should use the opportunity to convey the company's values, and should be prepared and able to give people feedback or on-the-spot help. The following are a few things that effective leaders do when they are on their ground zero walks:

- Talk to process associates, frontliners, janitors, salesmen, and so on

- Talk to customers and get their views on how the organization can serve them better

- Observe the way a process functions

- Observe how company employees interact with customers

- Be a part of a sales call

- Be a part of the team that addresses customer grievances

- Visit the restrooms that are used by customers

- Climb up and check the condition of the attic or roof

- Meet up with partners

- Observe what types of unseen wastes may be getting generated during process execution

During these ground zero walks, the focus should also be on understanding the things beyond the obvious, such as noticing the body language of the employees, hearing their comments, and gauging the general excitement of the employees with regard to LMS implementation. It is often a good idea for the entire top management team to each spend one day per month on ground zero walks, which could include meeting with customers. This can actually have a huge impact on the lean journey. If the leadership team has 10 members including the chief executive and they decide to each spend one day per month on ground zero walks, this would mean spending 10 days getting to know what's happening at the places of action. This can be extremely powerful for the company when the actions emanating from the ground zero walks are implemented. Suddenly, 10 different perspectives will come up on bettering the health of the lean management system and the larger organization as well.

Ground zero walks give a clear signal to the employees that leadership is serious about lean implementation and wants to know themselves what's happening in the workplace. However, ground zero walks may not deliver results if the leaders do not know what to do and look for. It is advisable that the chief improvement officer act as a coach for leaders who need to be guided on this.

The following are a few guidelines that should be followed during ground zero walks:

- Reserve one day per month for ground zero walks.

- The ground zero walks should be done not only by the chief executive but by the entire leadership team.

- During the walks, leaders should also review progress of the implementation of the lean management system in the workplace.

- The CEO should randomly pop into the offices of the senior management team and ask the inhabitants why they aren't out.

- Appear relaxed as you make your rounds. Employees will reflect your feelings and actions. Remain open and responsive to questions and concerns.

- Look for symptoms of potential problems and try to look beyond the obvious

- During the ground zero walks, try to find out whether necessary information is being passed on by operating managers on their workplace, processes, and quality.

- Talk with employees about their passions—whether family, hobbies, vacations, or sports.

Convey the image of a coach—not an inspector—and encourage your employees to open up. Try and discover the intent behind what is being said.

Daily Meetings

This is a process that needs to be institutionalized in any organization implementing lean. Daily meetings provide a platform wherein teams meet on a regular basis to discuss issues pertaining to the performance of the workplace. These are stand-up meetings that should be held once every day at a fixed time. The following items can be discussed during the daily meetings:

- Burning issues in the workplace
- Barriers to LMS implementation
- Introductions of new people
- Customer complaints
- Process bottlenecks
- Observed abnormalities in the workplace
- Review of measures of performance of processes, people, outputs, and outcomes
- Previous day's quality issues
- Capability-building progress
- Regulatory concerns
- Interpersonal issues between employees
- Communication on organizational changes
- Sharing of best practices
- New process introductions or changes
- Cost of poor quality
- Concerns pertaining to inventory levels, housekeeping, or cleanliness

Some of the above issues will be discussed daily while the others may be covered once a week or fortnight. It is recommended that a schedule for these issues be established. Exhibit 3.2 details a format that you can follow to generate a schedule.

The most senior person in the office should always conduct these daily meetings. This is to send a signal that it is important and everyone has to be a part of it.

I have found that the daily meeting has a tacit benefit in disciplining the employees. In an office in Singapore where I was facilitating the implementation of lean, the daily meetings forced the employees to be punctual. The offices started work at 9:00 AM and when the branch manager started convening these meetings at 9:00 AM, all habitual latecomers were forced to get to work on time to avoid embarrassment.

Topics discussed daily	Topics discussed less often

Date: _____

Ver: 1

Exhibit 3.2   Format of agenda for daily meeting.

Lessons to Ponder . . .

Daily meetings should be stand-up meetings only. The daily meetings should be stand-up meetings. Nobody likes to stand for long. Hence stand-up meetings have a huge benefit in that they force the meeting to be concluded in about 10 minutes. Also, when employees meet while standing, it becomes difficult for them to deny that they are part of the team.

PARTNERS

Partners are external entities whose efforts contribute to the performance of the organization. Partners could either be suppliers of inputs (raw materials) or they could be hired by the organization to provide specific services.

Following are the various types of partners who could be associated with the value streams of organizations:

- *Vendors.* Suppliers of inputs to processes, such as raw materials, consumables, and so on.

- *Process partners.* Outsourced agencies that run specific processes for a company or provide specific services, such as:

  - Direct marketing agencies used for business acquisition

  - Call centers for managing customer service requests

  - Collection agencies

  – Vendors used for processing credit cards

  – Vendors who manage the IT help desk of an organization.

As we shall see later, partners can either be a part of a process flow in a value stream or provide support to the processes in a value stream.

Irrespective of the standing of external partners with respect to processes, the organization needs to ensure that they are not allowed to manage their processes.

When applying lean, ensure that it touches the processes that are run by outsourced partners or vendors. Application of lean should be done to the end-to-end process without missing any stakeholders. For example, in the mortgage sanctions process shown in Figure 3.5, lean should be applied from *lead generation* to *disbursement to customers*. In this example, credit processing has been outsourced. When applying lean, ensure that activities in credit processing, though outsourced, are included in the transformation. This is to ensure that the desired impact of the transformation is felt.

Include the employees of vendors and outsourced agencies in all capability-building programs. Ensure that all the interventions that touch your organization also touch these entities.

Partner identification and engagement has to be driven by senior members of the company. Delegating this responsibility to a person who is low in the organization hierarchy and does not understand the larger picture can be futile. So the responsibility should be taken up by a senior member of the organization supported by a team of sourcing experts. The following are a few points that should be kept in mind in partner engagement:

- The partnership should be able to improve the organization's ability to serve the customer better or help in achieving other strategic objectives

- The partnership should aid in improving the competitiveness of the company

- Engaging a partner should be done keeping in mind the impact it will have on the end-to-end value stream

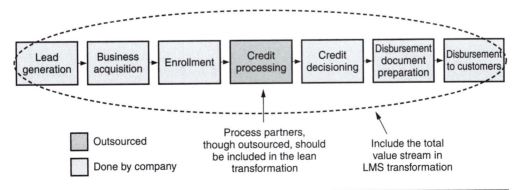

Figure 3.5   Process partner in a mortgage sanction process.

- Listen to the voice of the customer to understand the weaknesses of the company and seek partners to strengthen them

- Work out the total cost of the partnership and compare the before and after value cost

- Provide the partner access to company information

- There should be a high level of real-time visibility into the partnering process

- Ascertain the potential risks associated with outsourcing particular processes, grade them according to severity, and establish clear mitigants

- Establish a service-level agreement that clearly states the metrics that will be tracked

- Regularly carry out process walks to identify likely wastes and ascertain compliance levels

- Review the performance of the partner on a monthly basis, provide feedback, and work on improvement initiatives together

- On a quarterly basis, the management of both organizations should meet to share information, review performance, and share new products or offerings

- Train partner employees on relevant skills and competencies

- Share and cross-pollinate best practices

- Help in establishing a business continuity plan for the partner

- Ascertain process efficiency levels every quarter

PROBLEM SOLVING

A journey of lean transformation requires an equitable focus on implementation of both small improvement projects and large improvement projects. Quite often companies only focus their efforts on large projects that generate benefits through cost-efficiency and revenue enhancement. There is nothing wrong in this except that the approach is incomplete. We'll discuss this further. However, before we go ahead let us broadly understand what comprises large improvement projects and small improvement projects.

Large Improvement Projects (LIP)

These are large cross-functional projects focusing on key processes to deliver benefits to the bottom line. These projects take up to three to four months to complete and are implemented by experts on lean. These projects are driven by senior leaders and require the participation of a team represented by all stakeholders such as process, product, policy, risk, information technology, and so on. These projects have an objective to bring about a sea change in the way processes currently perform in the company. These projects are sponsored and led by top management or middle management.

Small Improvement Projects (SIP)

These are short-duration projects, to be completed within two to three weeks, that are implemented by associates working on the shop floor using elementary quality improvement tools. The target of these projects is to address local issues that never hit the radar of the leaders driving large projects. These projects have a major objective to garner involvement of the employees in improvements and also build a culture of improvements *by the employees, for the employees, of the employees.* The department or function leaders, who may be a part of the junior management team, sponsor these projects.

The major differences between large and small improvement projects are shown in Table 3.4

Table 3.5 gives examples of projects that fall into the categories of either large projects or small projects.

Table 3.4 Differences between large improvement projects and small improvement projects.

Details	Large improvement projects	Small improvement projects
Duration	Two to six months	Two to three weeks
Team size	Six to 10 people	Three to six people
Investments	May require major investment, including in technology	Require little or no investment
Pace	Small steps	Large steps
Sponsor	Senior management or middle management	Junior management
Team complexion	Assembled around a methodology expert Cross-functional teams	Cross-functional teams
Involvement	Everybody	Select few people
Tools	Six Sigma, TRIZ, advanced lean, DOE, Taguchi method, information technology	Seven QC tools or elementary tools of quality
Focus of outcomes	Impact on strategic business objectives such as costs, revenues, customers	Local issues of a workplace or process

Table 3.5 Examples of large and small improvement projects.

Number	Type of project	Sponsor	Example
1	Large improvement projects	Top management	Improving the way the mortgage business is done by moving from brick-and-mortar model to leveraging multiple channels
2		Middle management	Reduction of end-to-end disbursement lead times of mortgage processing
3	Small improvement projects	Junior management	Increasing the productivity of processing associates in a credit shop

Confluence of Large and Small Improvement Projects

Both large and small improvement projects are endowed with some inherent strengths that complement each other and are a must for building a solid improvement fabric in the company. Large projects are done on critical business processes of the organization while small projects target local workplace issues and small work processes and procedures. The beauty of small projects is that they do not require large investments and help in building a solid foundation of quality by rooting a culture of continual improvement. The employees implement them voluntarily to address specific issues impacting their workplace, for their own benefit. When organizations focus only on large projects, improvements are performed by a set of experts who simply arrive and carry out the improvements. In the eyes of the individuals on the shop floor, large-project implementation is about individuals like lean mavens swooping into their workplace like extra-terrestrials, facilitating a set of solutions, and then flying out. To them, they are adopting something that has been initiated by someone else, which they then have to internalize. Furthermore, it could appear to be an improvement that has been forced on them and requires their ongoing maintenance and sustaining. Remember, improvements that are pushed by someone else and have been adopted in a half-hearted manner won't be sustained but will deteriorate. Even if there is a high degree of acceptance of such solutions, the chances of the system degrading over a period of time are high. Given this context, it is imperative that all large projects are backed with a large number of small projects that are led and implemented by the associates working in the processes on the shop floor. This implies that one large project should be associated with or followed by a large number of small projects. I call this the LIP–SIP construct of improvements (see Figure 3.6).

For the larger organization, this means a Deming wheel of improvement embedded with large and small improvement projects functioning in the company (see Figure 3.7).

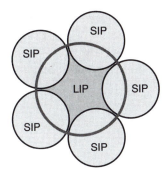

Figure 3.6 The LIP–SIP construct of improvements.

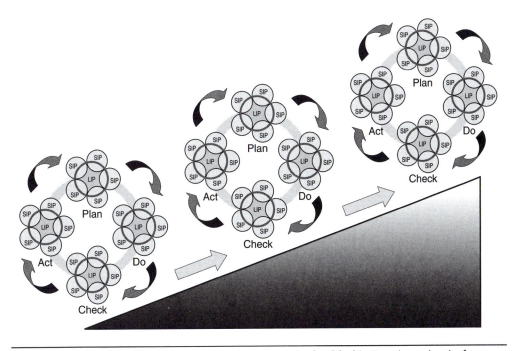

Figure 3.7 Small and large improvement projects embedded in Deming wheel of improvement in the company.

Results of the Confluence of Large and Small Improvement Projects

The other important perspective worth noting is how the confluence of both small and large projects creates a rhythm of continual improvement in the company. Let's understand this further by looking at Figure 3.8. Large projects lead to a quantum leap in

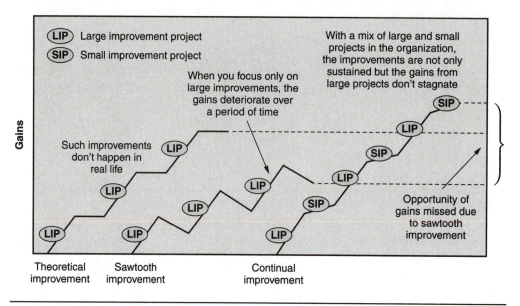

Figure 3.8 Theoretical, sawtooth, and continual improvement.

the way we operate while small projects bring about incremental improvements. It is normally believed that if we carry out large improvements in the organization, they will be sustained until we commence with the next round of improvement. Unfortunately this is a theoretician's perspective on improvement and in real life does not happen. What normally happens is that even the best of gains from large projects deteriorate over a period of time, leading to what is called *sawtooth improvement*. As a result, the benefits that should have been reaped from the project do not get delivered to the organization. However, when large projects are backed up by small projects, the gains are not only sustained but there is an incremental improvement even within the gains. Over a period of time, the overall quality bar of the company is raised. Compare this with the lost opportunity due to sawtooth improvement.

Epilogue

To summarize, both large and small improvement projects are essential to the LMS journey of the organization. Lean deployment should include strategies to roll out both in parallel. While large projects bring about quantum leaps in performance levels, small projects result in incremental improvements. Unlike large projects, which emerge from the upper echelons of the organizational hierarchy, small projects are initiated, owned, and implemented by the teams who work on the shop floor. The endeavor of companies should be to reach a state where employees are motivated enough to regularly initiate improvement projects. Of course, this is not easy and requires a facilitating environment wherein employees are regularly trained on basic problem-solving tools and encouraged to initiate small projects. However, this process is organic in nature and takes time, so leaders need to be patient.

Improvement Vault

Selecting the right improvement projects is critical to an organization's journey to lean transformation. I have seen companies wherein large numbers of projects are implemented but they do not create the desired impact to the organization. All that one hears is that improvement projects are being executed but no one really gets to see the tangible gains from these efforts.

If this continues to happen for some time, the lean journey will be seen as an overhead that creates a lot of hype but does not add value to the business. The participation of employees will be cosmetic and improvements will not get the attention of the senior leadership. Improvements will not have linkage to business objectives and they will be carried out in isolation.

Selecting the right projects for improvement is one of the critical factors for the success of lean implementation in a company. So, how does one ensure that projects that are initiated create the required impact to the organization? To achieve this, it is recommended that a central repository be created called the *improvement vault* (see Figure 3.9).

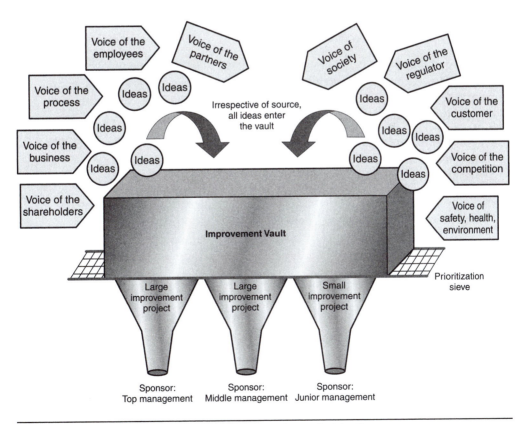

Figure 3.9 Improvement vault and idea-to-project prioritization.

So, what is an improvement vault? An improvement vault is a place wherein all potential ideas for improvements are logged irrespective of the source.

What kind of ideas? Ideas are issues, problems, or opportunities that need to be worked on. They may be problems that require resolution. But "problems" should not be taken as something negative for the organization. but rather an opportunity for improvement. So a problem could be a new product development or could be about resolving a customer complaint.

Further, it should be noted that ideas can either be proactive or reactive in nature. Proactive ideas are those that are initiated in anticipation of an event; reactive ideas are those that are implemented after an event has happened.

The improvement ideas come in from the various voices that surround a business, which comprise the following:

- *Voice of the customer.* These ideas typically concern complaints, feedback, and other inputs received from the customer.

- *Voice of the shareholder.* These ideas come from the company owners and investors in the company. They also include ideas that emerge from the corporate governance process.

- *Voice of the partners.* These are improvement ideas that come from vendors and partners, who may either be doing work for the organization or could be supplying inputs to processes.

- *Voice of the employees.* These are ideas that come from the employees of the company. The company should have a process to ensure that all employees giving ideas are responded to as to what is being done with them. Even if no actions are taken, the company should get back to them saying so.

- *Voice of the process.* These are ideas that emerge from the performance of processes. These could be both leading and lagging indicators. The process dashboard is typically the source of this "voice."

- *Voice of the business.* These ideas typically emanate from the imperatives and drivers of the business. These also include the strategic objectives, consisting of things such as financial numbers and customer, process, and internal capability targets.

- *Voice of the regulator.* These are ideas that are triggered by specific requirements of regulators. All such ideas should be viewed as a top priority as failure to do so could negatively impact the business. The voice of the regulator also includes all specific laws of the land.

- *Voice of the competition.* These are ideas triggered by happenings on the competitor's end. Organizations should have a robust process to gather competitive intelligence. This includes changes that may be happening in other industries that could be impacting the industry in which the company operates.

- *Voice of society.* These are potential project ideas triggered by the company's responsibility toward the society in which they operate.

- *Voice of safety, health, and environment.* This includes all ideas that have an impact on the safety and health of employees and also the environment in which the company operates.

Irrespective of the source, all ideas enter the improvement vault. They are stored and are "pushed through a sieve" to prioritize them. The improvement vault can be software-based, which facilitates idea storage and subsequent prioritization. The "sieve" is a decision rule engine that allows prioritization using project selection criteria, which can be stipulated by the organization. The criteria could include parameters such as importance, problem type, urgency, and organizational, customer, business, or regulatory impact. The project selection criteria can be changed based on changes in business context and requirements.

The ideas are prioritized as follows:

- Large improvement project sponsored by top management

- Large improvement project sponsored by middle management

- Small improvement projects sponsored by junior management

These have been discussed in detail previously.

High-Impact Projects

It is important to understand what constitutes a high-impact project. Defining this can not be done in haste and requires inputs from across functions. It has to be carefully thought through and holistic enough to comprise all the shades of improvement that are taken up by the organization. An incomplete definition of what comprises a high-impact project is often a reason why projects do not deliver the requisite value. This is important because organizations can't afford to squander their expensive resources such as lean mavens on only average projects. So, what are high-impact projects?

The following are brief guidelines that companies can follow to identify ideas that are potential high-impact projects:

- *Projects that facilitate achievement of strategic objectives.* These projects directly impact the performance of the company and are a part of the performance scorecard used by the top management team such as the CEO, functional heads, value stream owners, and so on. Examples of such projects include those targeted toward achievement of favorable business numbers such as revenue, market share, volumes, economic value added, return on capital employed, and so on.

- *Projects that build core competency.* These projects help in building the core competency of a business by building capabilities that help to better the way business is managed in the company. For example, implementing a wing-to-wing project to improve the disbursement turnaround times of an automobile financing business. This also includes projects that address concerns pertaining to employee retention, innovation, empowerment, technology, communication, reliability, and so on. These projects often impact issues that build the internal capabilities of the organization.

- *Projects that impact operational efficiencies.* These projects are targeted toward better utilization of resources by the business. Resources include manpower, material, machines, methods, and milieu.

Projects taken up for efficiency improvement, waste elimination, resource optimization, and productivity elevation all fall in this group. These projects typically lead to significant cost reductions and lead to green or blue savings.

Green savings are real cash savings visible in the accounting system that can be reinvested by the company. Green savings happen due to the reduction in manpower, materials, transportation cost, vendors, non-profitable customers, productivity improvement, and so on.

Blue savings are not necessarily visible in the accounting system but are important for the company and include projects that result in benefits such as lead time reduction, improved organizational culture, improved product quality, and so on. Blue savings are not real cash and cannot be reinvested by the company.

- *Projects that impact chronic customer issues.* These projects are focused on addressing customer issues being faced by a business. The source of these projects is the voice of the customer, captured through approaches such as surveys, mystery shopping, feedback, complaints, service data, customer reviews, and focus group interviews.

Implementing a project to eliminate the recurring problem of bloated tuna cans is an example of such a project.

- *Projects that impact stakeholders.* These projects address problems with the partners who impact our stakeholders. These stakeholders include all interested parties who are a part of our business flow and include vendors (such as marketing agents, sales agents, product suppliers, and couriers), regulators, customers, and so on.

- *Projects that impact competitive position.* These ideas help improve the competitive position of the business. They are developmental in nature and include projects initiated to develop new products, processes, or services. Implementing a project to reinvent the way a mortgage business is done would fall into this category.

PROMOTIONS

Reward and Recognition for Lean

Reward and recognition (R&R) is an important anchor in an organization's lean transformation journey. The goal of an R&R program should be to reinforce the desired behaviors that drive improvement and promote the achievement of business objectives using lean. When employees know that their efforts are appreciated, it will increase their self-esteem and satisfaction.

Reward and recognition practices for LMS deployment broadly fall under two headings:

1. *Nonmonetary reward practices.* These are rewards that help to elevate the self-worth of individuals and teams. These rewards should be administered by the LMS office in association with the human resources department.

2. *Monetary reward practices.* These are rewards that impact the compensation of individuals and teams. They can be manifested as gain sharing, profit sharing, variable pay, or employee stock options.

I have seen that the nonmonetary rewards work best in a journey of lean implementation. While there are a number of nonmonetary schemes, I am presenting the ones that I have seen to be successful during LMS implementation (see Table 3.6).

Table 3.6   List of nonmonetary awards for LMS implementation.

Type of reward scheme	Description	Frequency	Level of hierarchy it targets
Publicity/ newsletters	In this form of recognition the name of the achiever is placed in a newsletter or on a notice board that is visible to the employees of the company. The biggest kick that the achiever gets is that his or her achievement is shared with peers/colleagues	Do it as many times as possible. Once a month is quite common	All levels but specifically junior and middle management
Epaulettes and badges	These are awards given spontaneously to recognize specific acts of individuals	As many times as possible	Junior and middle management
Restaurant passes/ movie tickets	These are team rewards that recognize the achievements made by the team. The winning team is given vouchers/passes for entertainment activities	Once a month	Junior and middle management

Continued

Table 3.6   List of nonmonetary awards for LMS Implementation. *(Continued)*

Type of reward scheme	Description	Frequency	Level of hierarchy it targets
Lunch with CEO	This is given to a work unit that has made major inroads to increase the consciousness of lean thinking in the workplace	Once in six months	Middle and junior management
Chief executive's award for LMS champ	This is given to individuals who demonstrate value that builds the lean management system in the organization. This should be targeted to individuals at top, middle, and junior management of the company	Once a year	Top, middle, and junior management
Chief executive's award for best value stream	This is an award given to the value stream that has instilled the majority of the elements of the lean management system	Once a year	Team and owner comprising value stream
Chief executive's award for best project	This is given to the team that has delivered the project that has had the maximum impact on the strategic objectives of the organization	Once a year	Teams at any level
The partnership award	This is given to the partner who has successfully achieved results using principles of lean	Once a year	Teams from partner organization
The behind-the-scenes leader award	This is given to a business leader who has made substantial contributions toward building the lean management system from behind the scenes	Once a year	Leadership team of the company
Best small improvement project	This award to given to the team that delivers the best small improvement project	Once a quarter	Junior management
The customer award	This award is given to the business unit or value stream that has achieved excellence in customer service	Once a quarter	Top, middle, and junior management
Best improvement project	This is given to the best lean improvement project delivered by a team, that has made a significant impact on business performance	Once a quarter	Middle and junior management

Try and present a mix of team as well as individual rewards. In a lean journey it is imperative that team awards are encouraged, to inspire teamwork and balanced performance. While individual achievers should be identified and recognized, the focus should be to bring out the point that team performance overarches individual performance.

Among monetary rewards, the author has seen that variable pay and employee stock options deliver the best results.

At the end of the day, organizations should choose the types of rewards based on the culture and context, and the behaviors that it would like to encourage. Install an effective and transparent measurement mechanism to decide the winners.

Problem Prevention Mind-Set

Evidence and precursors precede virtually all problems. These could take the form of either a "non-serious event," as a slight delay in serving a dish to the guests in a restaurant, or an "attention-grabbing incident," as an incorrect dish served to the customer. They both indicate the inevitable—that there is a problem that has still to be discovered. It is something like a tremor before an earthquake, or body aches preceding a fever, or an electric shock occurring before a major safety blowup.

In many organizations, problems are addressed only after they happen. Even after knowing the problem, it is often the symptoms of the problem and not the causes that are addressed; as a result the problems keep on repeating. Since the underlying causes are not identified and addressed, they continue to create recurring problems. Even with ongoing or increased efforts, the problems persist, performance is impacted, and frustration becomes the norm. Eventually, hopelessness and helplessness invade the organization's culture. The challenge before organizational leaders is to build a culture that promotes problem identification wherein employees do not wait for problems to happen but proactively look for signals that precede a problem. It is the duty of the top management, value stream owners, and chief improvement officer to repeatedly communicate the importance of *problem prevention* or identifying problems before they occur. Remember, this is not easy and takes time to become an integral part of the company's fabric. But one of the signs of successful lean implementation is when the bulk of the employees proactively look for signs of opportunities for improvement.

It may be useful to educate all employees on how to identify when problems are likely to happen in an organization. The following is a partial list of specific incidents that I have learned from the work of Gerald F. Smith that may indicate that problems are on the horizon:

- *Change event.* Whenever there are changes there is a likelihood that they could be followed by a problem.

- *Precursors.* Are there any precursors? This could be as simple as a machine getting hot before breaking down. Precursors may often appear to be nonserious.

- Is there any striking incident like the electric shock before a safety incident?

- Are incidents repeating? Is there is a pattern emerging from the incidents?

- Are there sudden complaints?

- Are your users experiencing problems with the products or services you are offering? Here you need to proactively seek feedback or get into the mind-frame of the user.

- Are there any surprising observations? These are anomalies that could result in major incidents. These are called *warusa kagen* in Japanese, or "things that are not problems but do not seem quite right." (Smith 2000)

The responsibility rests with the entire leadership team to inculcate the mind-set of problem prevention among the employees. Initiate improvement projects when symptoms are seen; don't wait for problems to happen. Leverage the power of lean projects for prevention.

Lessons to Ponder . . .

Encourage your employees to identify symptoms of potential problems that could be the focus of lean improvement projects.

Brown Bag Sessions

As you implement a lean management system in your organization it would make great sense to hold ongoing sessions on various lean concepts, tools, and techniques to continually educate the employees. This may also be helpful in that many questions pop up in the minds of the employees that they are afraid to ask the help desk for fear of being exposed. For example, a lean breakthrough program may just tell participants the formula for takt time calculation but may not delve into its application under varied process settings. Participants may want to know how to apply this concept in settings such as processes churning multiple products, seasonal variation, month-end peak loads, and so on. This is where *brown bag sessions* can be very handy. A brown bag session is a powerful tool to successfully educate large number of employees on a given topic. This tool is also required for team members who have not undergone exhaustive lean maven classroom sessions.

What is a brown bag session? A "brown bag" is an inexpensive educational session conducted during breakfast, lunch, or snacks for employees keen on knowing more about lean. The sessions are conducted by the employees and meant for the employees. The objective of this tool is to help employees with concepts of lean and the tools involved without having them complete off-site training. These sessions are voluntary, so they should be made attractive by offering a nice lunch or array of snacks. You could even distribute books or cassettes on relevant topics to act as an incentive for the attendee. A lean maven, or any other person in the company who is adept in the topic under deliberation, takes employees through the concepts while they enjoy a bite. For example, a lean maven may conduct a session on layout design. Or a branch banking process owner may be told to prepare a topic (say, "wastes in a bank branch") that he or she could share during a brown bag. I have tried this successfully in the past and it usually yields huge results.

The following is a list of guidelines that you should follow for successful execution of a brown bag session:

- Schedule one- to two-hour meetings on a regular basis (every week or every fortnight).

- Please do not cut costs here. Give them something to eat. If not lunch, at least some snacks.

- Focus on time is a must. Do not make the sessions too long. Ensure that they are completed within the stipulated time. Remember, if the session is too long, people will not attend such sessions in the future.

- Make sure that senior management team members attend a few of these brown bags, especially when you launch the initiative.

- Do not make the sessions too theoretical. The concepts should be laced with real-life examples.

When you launch your brown bag sessions, the attendance may be poor. Do not get perturbed. Keep having the brown bags and do a good job. Soon, word of mouth will spread and attendance will increase.

Lessons to Ponder . . .

Brown bag sessions increase the knowledge of employees on lean and its associated tools and techniques at a minimum cost.

A3 Promotion

An organization implementing lean should institutionalize the use of the *A3 template*. This a brilliant tool that can be used for two purposes: problem solving and strategy deployment.

A3 for Problem Solving and Continual Improvement. This application is about capturing all the details of an improvement project on a single piece of paper. These are written on a piece of paper of size 11" × 17", hence the name A3 reports. The format of the report is such that it provides a structure for carrying out improvements in an effective manner. These reports are displayed in the workplace where the improvement is being carried out so that it is not only visible to all but so that teams know exactly what has to be done or has gone into resolving a problem. Whether it is a large improvement project or a small improvement project, this template should be religiously used by an

A3 Report—Problem Solving   Date: _____

Name of the company: _____ Business unit: _____ Workplace: _____

Project name: _____ Project ID: _____ Team leader: _____ Team members: _____

Business case/backdrop:	Future state:
Objectives:	
Current state:	Detailed action plan:

Detailed action plan:

What	When	Who	How

Barriers to implementation:

Before and after metrics

Parameters	Before	After	Remarks

Review dates:

What to review	Who reviews	Where	When

Sustainability imperatives:

Signature of team leader _____   No: _____ Ver: 1

Exhibit 3.3   A3 template for problem solving/improvement projects.

organization implementing lean. Exhibit 3.3 shows a typical template used for this purpose. The content of the A3 report not only brings focus to meetings but also reduces the number of and time spent on meetings. The A3 template helps to institutionalize a common approach to problem solving that can be followed and understood by the entire company. The movement toward waste reduction should not just be within processes but also incorporated into the information presented for improvement projects. The A3 template shuns verbosity and ensures that the entire project is captured and documented in a crisp, concise manner. Building a culture of using A3 templates is not an easy task and requires all employees to be coached on the tool. The ownership of institutionalizing A3 templates rests with the lean maven. Leaders should review improvement projects in no format other than the A3 template, and this should also hold true in the workplace where the project is being implemented.

A3 for Strategy Deployment. The A3 template can also be used by teams at all levels of the organization to capture the work plan for a year. This could either emanate from the balanced scorecard, which has been discussed earlier, or through an exercise of policy deployment (*hoshin kanri*). The A3 template clearly states the objectives for the current year, a reflection of last year's work, and detailed action plan. Leaders at all levels of the company, starting with the CEO on down to team leaders, should use the A3 template to encapsulate their work plan. Leaders should get into the habit of expressing their work plan in one page and not get into long and fancy presentations. The construct of the template for strategy deployment is shown in Exhibit 3.4. The A3 design has an intuitive, logical flow that allows the entire story to be told in 15 to 20 minutes with all likely questions having been answered. For additional detail I would recommend the book *Getting the Right Things Done: A Leader's Guide to Planning and Execution* by Pascal Dennis.

A3 Report—Strategy Deployment   Date: _____

Name of the company: _____ Business unit: _____ Department: _____

Team leader: _____ Year under review: _____

Last year's performance:

Detailed action plan:

What	When	Who	How

Reflection of last year's performance:

Critical success factors:

Current year's objectives:

Before and after metrics

Parameters	Before	After	Remarks

Justification for this year's focus area:

Issues pending to be resolved:

Signature of team leader _____   No: _____ Ver: 1

Exhibit 3.4   A3 template for strategy deployment.

Lessons to Ponder . . .

Leaders implementing lean in their organization should be in a position to capture their work plan in a single piece of paper. If they are not able to do so, they are probably not aware of the larger picture and the context in which the business objectives have been set.

Value Stream Thinking

This is about inculcating among all the employees the mind-set of thinking about the outcome of the total value stream. This entails redirecting their efforts beyond functional or departmental goals to the larger process goals. This means building a culture wherein individuals and teams appreciate that at times functional goals need to be sacrificed for the larger effectiveness of the process. Under this philosophy, individuals cutting across functions work together as a team to achieve the common value stream objectives.

Everybody in the company is sensitized to how improvements impact the entire value stream. A culture of value stream thinking instills a process thinking mind-set where any time there is a problem in the workplace the first thing done is to look into the causal process responsible for it. Individuals are not held responsible for problems but endeavor to correct the processes that made them happen. While injecting the DNA of value stream thinking into the workforce, make sure that employees understand the basics of process management, which comprise value-added/non-value-added, inputs, outputs, resources, constraints, and metrics (leading and lagging). At the end of the day, you need to create a company wherein employees realize, practice, and leverage the power of processes. A team's solitary goal is to work together to create value for the customer.

Lessons to Ponder . . .

• In a lean organization, employees may set aside narrow goals for the larger objective of the value stream.

• Before setting out to change the culture of the organization, focus on transforming the company systems and processes of the selected pilot project.

4

Lean Breakthroughs

In its journey to LMS implementation, an organization needs to master the art of carrying out *lean breakthrough* improvement projects. Traditionally carried out in automobile companies, lean breakthroughs can be very successfully applied to service companies. The author has personally facilitated more than 100 breakthroughs in a large financial services conglomerate.

As the organization progresses on the journey of lean transformation, lean breakthroughs bring "life" to the deployment. They not only ensure involvement of teams but also help to deliver quick results. The power of the lean breakthrough can not be appreciated until one participates in it.

Also called a *kaizen blitz* (as named by the Association of Manufacturing Excellence, USA), a lean breakthrough aims at a spectacular improvement over a short period of time in a focused area using a dedicated team. Remember, if the results are less than spectacular it is not a lean breakthrough. Popularized by individuals such as Masaaki Imai, James Womack (author of *Lean Thinking*), and the Association of Manufacturing Excellence, the lean breakthrough is not so much about planning but rather acting on problems now. It is about "learning by doing." A lean breakthrough session begins with a training session for the team members who will implement what they have learned, resolving the problem within five to seven days. A lean breakthrough happens with the involvement of an empowered set of individuals who can take any necessary decisions pertaining to the change. Lean breakthroughs are called *kaikaku* in Japanese. Literally translating as "instant revolution," this tool, like many other improvement concepts, emanated from the Toyota company, where it is used for waste elimination on the shop floor.

With the objective of facilitating an effective lean breakthrough, I have worked out an approach that will come in very handy for individuals keen on adopting this improvement vehicle. The steps are summarized in Figure 4.1.

The lean breakthrough comprises three phases: (1) preparation, (2) action, and (3) follow-up.

Let's examine the details of each of these phases.

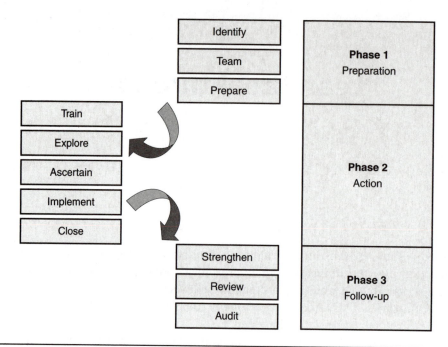

Figure 4.1   Steps in a lean breakthrough.

PHASE 1: PREPARATION

This is the phase when planning for the lean breakthrough is carried out. It comprises preparations that need to be done before actually executing the breakthrough. This is a very important phase as a lot of preparation is required before the actual action. Lean breakthroughs often fail because of inadequate planning. This phase comprises three steps, which are as follows.

Identify

In this step the problem is identified. This is typically done by the LMS office, who prioritizes the problems that come out of the improvement vault and pass them on to the lean maven in the business unit where the problem lies. As a part of the identification process, the LMS office broadly defines the problem, which is refined further by the lean maven. Remember, a sharp definition of the problem gives clear direction on where the potential for action lies and what needs to be done. It also tells you the types of team members required for the lean breakthrough.

Selecting a problem of strategic importance to the organization is a must. You can choose a product, process, or work area, depending on the context and type of problem. However, be cognizant of the fact that whatever area you select to focus on should be amenable to a lean breakthrough. Do not choose a management problem; choose an operating problem.

Team

Having defined the problem, the lean maven facilitates team selection. Putting together an appropriate team is critical to the success of a lean breakthrough. Typically, the team size should be anywhere from eight to fourteen individuals. The composition should be a mix of individuals from the work area impacted by the lean breakthrough, from outside the department, and even customers or suppliers. It is important to have individuals with lots of new ideas and a "can do" attitude. Select an individual with good facilitation skills and participatory management style as the team leader. To avoid bias, he or she should preferably not be a person from the work area. The lean maven should never be the team leader, acting instead as a facilitator of the entire process. In financial services companies, a lean breakthrough should have compulsory representatives from departments such as information technology, risk, and compliance. The team members will spend all their time on this project during the five days of the breakthrough.

Prepare

A lot of preparation needs to be done before launching a lean breakthrough. This begins with a communication that is sent to the all the value stream stakeholders who will be impacted by the lean breakthrough. Clearly convey the business case and goals associated with the breakthrough, how its fits into the overall improvement strategy of the organization, and how the intervention will deliver long-term benefits despite short-term work disruption. Since there could be a change in layouts, process flow, or equipment, inform all the contractors, vendors, and IT experts who would need to be present during the blitz. If the organization has a union, it may be required to align with them. Assure all concerned that there will be no layoffs as a result of the breakthrough event. And do not forget to photograph the area before the commencement of the event.

PHASE 2: ACTION

In this phase the actual breakthrough is carried out; teams go to the workplace and actually deliver the solution. This phase consists of the steps summarized in Table 4.1. Table 4.2 shows an approach followed when doing a lean breakthrough for sales.

Train

Before the team gets into the lean breakthrough, the team members go through a half-day training program that should comprise topics such as basics of lean, types of wastes, 5S,

Table 4.1 Typical schedule for a five-day lean breakthrough.*

Day of the week	Steps**	Details
Monday	Train	Basic training, align on the objectives, tour the work area, process walk, time observation, data analysis
Tuesday	Explore	Waste identification, value stream mapping, spaghetti diagram, process baselining (lead time, defects/errors, first-pass yield, customer service, productivity, process efficiency), takt time calculation
Wednesday	Ascertain	Improvement opportunities, root cause identification, manpower numbers (actual versus new), new process and layout design, alignment with all stakeholders, competency mapping, process manual, role redefinition, load balancing
Thursday	Implement	Training of associates, new process rollout, implement countermeasures, install new measurements, 5S
Friday	Close	New process up and running, training complete, SOPs functional, comparison of as-is/to-be metrics, action plan for next 30 days, wrap-up presentation to leadership, celebration

 * Number of days could also be 6 to 7
** There could be some overlap between the steps

Table 4.2 Typical schedule for a five-day lean breakthrough for improving sales force productivity.*

Day of the week	Steps**	Details
Monday	Train	Basic training, align on the objectives, process walk, expectation analysis, interview of key stakeholders, product understanding, time observation, data analysis
Tuesday	Explore	Waste identification, value stream mapping, spaghetti diagram, process baselining (lead time, defects/errors, first-pass yield, customer service, productivity, process efficiency), takt time calculation, compensation structure, competency analysis
Wednesday	Ascertain	Variable identification in process (input/output matrix), variable prioritization, brainstorming with leadership team, a day in the life of _____, role profiling, improvement opportunities, root cause identification, manpower numbers (actual versus new), new process and layout design, alignment with all stakeholders, competency mapping, process manual, role redefinition, load balancing
Thursday	Implement	Training of associates, new process rollout, implement countermeasures, install new measurements, 5S, sales pitch, new job description, sales FAQs, recruitment process, performance management system
Friday	Close	New process up and running, training complete, comparison of as-is/to-be metrics, action plan for next 30 days, wrap-up presentation to leadership, celebration

 * Number of days could also be 6 to 7
** There could be some overlap between the steps

PDCA (plan–do–check–act) cycle, takt time, value-added/non-value-added/business-value-added, visual controls, elementary problem solving (using the seven QC tools), spaghetti diagram, standard work sheet, and lean simulation game. After the training, the participants may still have a lot questions on the lean tools but do not worry. Many of these will be answered during the breakthrough when the teams are actually a part of the action.

Explore

In this step the team explores the problems and tries to reveal the as-is state. In this step the endeavor is to understand the problem better, which is accomplished through a process walk, baselining of the process, as-is data analysis, waste analysis, and takt time calculation.

Ascertain

In this step the team gets into the root cause of the problem and finding potential solutions. This step typically includes brainstorming, root cause analysis, manpower study, load balancing, new process and layout design, competency analysis, role redefinition, process manual, and stakeholder alignment. The outcome of this step is a construct of the new process, which is ready to be rolled out.

Implement

This step comprises implementing all the solutions that were arrived at in the previous step. In this step the bulk of the team members are a part of the action in the workplace. This broadly comprises (a) training of process associates, (b) redesignation of roles, (c) rollout of new process, (d) measurement, (e) 5S deployment. The author has seen 5S deployment to be an integral part of many lean breakthrough projects. By the end of this step the new process is up and running and the improvement is demonstrated to all stakeholders. The improved process is handed over to the process owner. Often, accomplishment of this step leads to changing the complexion of the workplace due to the new process and layout. At the end of this step a photograph is often taken to show the difference between the earlier workplace and the new one.

Close

Having completed the implementation, the teams work toward closing the project. This includes making a presentation for the leadership team and also working out the 30-day action plan (Exhibit 4.1). It is quite possible that all action points may not get implemented over the five days of the breakthrough; if not, they are included in the 30-day action plan. Over the next 30 days all the action points and countermeasures need to be implemented. However, it may be noted that the bulk of the actions should be implemented within the five days; only a few should be a part of the 30-day action plan. The

				Inputs required (State names of individuals from whom inputs will be taken)	Investment required** (Clearly state the likely investments required)	
What (action points)	**Who**	**When**	**How**			**Review dates**

Date: _____

Problem definition: _____

Dates of lean breakthrough: _____ Process owner: _____ Lean maven: _____

Ver: 1

Exhibit 4.1 Template for 30-day action plan.

content of the presentation is shown in Exhibit 4.2. After the presentation to the leadership, the team typically has a get-together to cross-pollinate learnings and celebrate the successful implementation. Having handed over the process to the process owner, the team is disbanded and the members go back to their respective workplaces.

PHASE 3: FOLLOW-UP

This phase is dedicated to post-implementation actions. It involves completion of all the residual steps so that the project can be completed in all respects and also entails putting together a mechanism to sustain the gains. There are three steps in this phase, as follows.

Strengthen

This entails completing the 30-day action plan that had been scripted in the earlier phase. The teams associated with the process typically lead the implementation of these action points. The lean maven provides input on lean tools and techniques. A tracker is also put in place by the lean maven to track the progress of the action points. This is an absolute imperative as the author has often seen that without a tracking regimen, actions do not get closed out.

Date: _____

Content of a lean breakthrough closing presentation:

1. Objective of the project
2. Team members
3. Daily schedule and approach followed
4. Business case
5. As-is value stream map/process map
6. As-is metrics
7. Spaghetti diagram
8. Waste analysis
9. Overview of calculations
10. To-be value stream map/process map
11. Root causes and key solutions implemented
12. As-is versus new layout
13. As-is versus to-be load balancing chart
14. Before and after photos
15. Metrics before and after
16. 30-day action plan
17. Learnings

Ver: 1

Exhibit 4.2   Typical content of a lean breakthrough closing presentation.

Review

The process owner reviews the progress of the action plans in the presence of the lean maven. To ensure that actions are closed out, a stand-up review thrice a week often helps. This is because closing out all action points within 30 days can be quite a challenge if proper focus is not applied.

Audit

After the 30-day action plan is completed, and the project has been closed, it is important that the process is audited on a regular basis. We have discussed process audits earlier. To ensure that the gains are sustained, the process should be audited at least once a quarter. It is important that the process owner take the audits seriously. He or she can use the template shown in Exhibit 4.3 to track the audits.

Lean breakthrough (number)	Name of the process	Process ID	Process owner	Audit frequency				Remarks
				Qtr 1	Qtr 2	Qtr 3	Qtr 4	

Date: _____

Ver: 1

Exhibit 4.3   Template for managing audits of the process in which a lean breakthrough has been carried out.

Learnings from Lean Breakthroughs

The following are a few things that need to be remembered for lean breakthroughs:

- Selecting the right team is key for the lean breakthrough. Avoid choosing members who are lazy and shun hard work.

- Before commencing with the lean breakthrough, align with the process owner. Solicit his or her views, if any, on what their expectations are of the project.

- Inform all the stakeholders who are going to be impacted by the project. Tell them that there could be some disruption but when they see the results they will realize that it was worth it.

- Select problems with sharp definition for lean breakthroughs.

- Avoid problems that cut across functions and locations. Lean breakthroughs are best for localized problems.

- After the value stream mapping is done for a process, a series of lean breakthroughs can help to migrate to the interim and future states.

- Clearly tell all members that the five days that they will be spending on the lean breakthrough will require a lot of hard work. There could be days when the activities will go until midnight or early morning.

- Tell the team members that during the five days there will be times when they will feel like giving up, but with grit and determination they will close out the project.

- The lean maven should never lead the project; someone else should always be the leader of the project. The lean maven should act like a coach during the entire project execution.

- During the early phases of the LMS journey, it is imperative that the leadership team should participate one by one in lean breakthroughs to see their power and results bias.

- Don't look for the perfect solution during the lean breakthrough. A quick and functional result is fine. However, the result has to be spectacular, which means results such as a 30 to 50 percent reduction in head count, 30 to 50 percent improvement in productivity, 70 percent reduction in error rates, and so on.

- During the five days it is a must that all daily action points are completed before closing the day.

- A cross-functional team is a must. Avoid having too many people from the workplace or process where the work will be happening. This is required to get an outside perspective.

- Clearly tell all the employees/associates that there will be no layoffs as a result of the lean breakthrough. At the most, associates may be redeployed to some other function, job, or process. Remember, if an organization uses lean breakthroughs to lay off people, it will be the end of the lean journey.

- The LMS office should ensure that an engine be put in place such that lean breakthroughs touch the length and breadth of the company.

- Sometimes it helps to have the chief financial officer as a member of the team to have financial benefits validated.

- Lean breakthroughs should be discussed at the level of top management once a quarter. It also helps to share with the top management one or two successful projects.

- In the early stages of implementation, all lean breakthroughs should have a lean maven. Once capability is attained within a business unit, the lean maven can simultaneously manage a number of lean breakthroughs.

- Together with the number of lean breakthrough projects implemented in a business unit, the focus should also be to monitor the *quality* of projects.

- Sometimes it helps to have a lean breakthrough dashboard for a business unit as shown in Exhibit 4.4. The value stream owner should review the dashboard every month.

- Lean breakthroughs help to build a continual improvement mind-set.

Number	Measurements	Status
	Date: _____	
1	Number of lean breakthrough projects done	
2	Benefits gathered from lean breakthrough projects	
3	Number of people participating in lean breakthrough	
4	Number of leaders participating in the projects	
5	Number of individuals identified who can lead	
6	Types of issues addressed by the lean breakthroughs	

Ver: 1

Exhibit 4.4   Lean breakthrough progress dashboard.

Lessons to Ponder . . .

Lean breakthroughs are such that they can spread like a fire and transform the improvement engine of an organization.

Appendix A

Assessment of the Lean Management System: The DEB-LOREX Index

OBJECTIVE

The objective of this instrument is to provide an overview of the status and health of the lean management system in an organization. It is based on the DEB-LOREX management system, which has been discussed earlier in the book.

HOW IT IS TO BE ADMINISTERED

The instrument is to be used for a selected organization or business unit. The assessor should run through the points and grade them based on their current status. The assessment should be carried out by a qualified LMS assessor who spends sufficient time in the target business unit to carry out the assessment. The process of assessment comprises interviews, performance measurements, and observations.

FREQUENCY

While no specific time frames can be specified, a reasonable timeline has to be given to close the gaps observed from the last assessment. It has been seen that there should be a gap of a minimum of three months between assessments.

WHAT DOES THE SCALE MEAN?

Rate each of the points on a scale of 1 to 5 where:

5 = Strongly agree

4 = Agree

3 = Neither agree nor disagree

2 = Disagree

1 = Strongly disagree

Summary Scores

Number	Areas		Maximum score (A)	Actual score (B)	Percent score C = (B)/(A) × 100
1	General				
2	Leadership				
3	Value stream				
4	Anchors	People			
		Processes			
		Partners			
		Problem solving			
		Promotions			
5	Customer				
6	Results				

Overall LMS Score

Number	Section		Weight in percentage* (W)	Percent received (C)	Actual score D = (W × C)/100
1	General				
2	Leadership				
3	Value stream				
4	Anchors	People			
		Processes			
		Partners			
		Problem solving			
		Promotions			
5	Customer				
6	Results				
	Total		100%		
DEB-LOREX Index = Σ (D1 + D2 + D3 ... D*n*) =					

*The weighting of each section can be decided by the organization.

1. General _____

Number	Points	1–5	Remarks
1	Lean to the company is about a holistic improvement journey that comprises making all the elements of the lean management system work in tandem to achieve the larger vision of the company		
2	The company is sensitive to the fact that lean is not just about tools and techniques but a philosophy for building operational excellence		
3	Operational excellence to the company is about bringing about customer convenience, revenue enhancement, and cost efficiency, and building a culture of continual improvement		
4	There is a general belief among the employees in the organization that even the best of processes, workplaces, and business systems contain opportunities for improvement		
5	Systems thinking is an integral part of the organizational fabric		
6	The interdependencies and interactions among processes and the components of the lean management system are known to all		
7	The organization manages the components of the lean management system in such a manner that it helps to deliver the vision crafted by the top leadership team and the board		
8	All employees are aware that change in any of the components of the system will affect the performance of the overall lean management system		
9	There is a continual endeavor to improve the overall effectiveness of the lean management system		
10	The components of the lean management system are managed in such a manner that people do the right things without being told		
11	The lean management system is not treated as separate from doing business; it is the business system		
12	The operating teams clearly understand the cause-and-effect relationship between the components of the lean management system and business results		
13	The company uses this assessment checklist to ascertain the health of the lean management system on an ongoing basis		
14	The company has institutionalized the LMS assessment process into a positive, engaging process in which leaders at all levels get involved		

2. Leadership

Number	Points	1–5	Remarks
1	The lean transformation in the organization is driven by the CEO		
2	The CEO and his or her direct reports are convinced that the lean management system has the necessary wherewithal to make a positive impact to the performance of the company		
3	A council comprising the CEO and his or her direct reports oversees the implementation of LMS		
4	The leadership team of the company is using lean as a strategy for business improvement and just not another quality methodology to be used by quality project teams		
5	The LMS council has set specific aspirational and future-state goals that need to be accomplished through the implementation of the lean management system		
6	The LMS council reviews progress of implementation at least once a month		
7	The organization has a vision, mission, and values that echo the principles of lean thinking		
8	The entire leadership team, comprising the CEO and his or her direct reports, understands the underlying principles of lean and its key drivers		
9	The leadership team demonstrates its commitment to the lean transformation by voluntarily investing time whenever required		
10	The leadership practices the principle of "customer first," which is not only about meeting the requirements of the end consumer but also the next person in the process (also called customers)		
11	The leaders know that successful implementation of lean is about successfully adopting and practicing LMS across the company and from top to bottom		
12	The chief executive spends at least one day in a month doing ground zero walks to get a feel for the area where the action is		
13	Leaders are driving lean to bring in overall organizational excellence and not just to cut costs		
14	Business leaders expect lean to deliver a large array of benefits such as revenue enhancement, service excellence, operational risk reduction, process efficiency, workplace safety, employee productivity, complexity reduction, and so on, over a period of time		

Continued

Continued

Number	Points	1–5	Remarks
15	The lean transformation is being looked at as a change management intervention and not just another methodology for improvements		
16	Each member of the leadership team and LMS council has participated in a lean breakthrough		
17	Leaders consistently seek to understand changing customer needs		
18	The leadership team regularly participates in communication sessions not only to share the company's performance but also to the energize the team to contribute to the lean movement		
19	The leadership team regularly communicates the importance of customer requirements and the role of the employees in connecting with the customer		
20	The CEO and the entire leadership team review the management report by the chief improvement officer and LMS office, which summarizes the overall health and status of implementation of the lean management system		
21	One of the areas that the company's leadership team emphasizes is building organization capability to sustain the lean movement built around the lean management system		
22	All the leaders know that companies are a collection of people who voluntarily come together for a purpose, so they have to be engaged and not mandated into the LMS process		
23	Leaders spend a lot of time coaching, mentoring, leading by example, and helping individuals to achieve their goals		
24	The leadership team constantly focuses on creating a new generation of leaders who understand and drive the principle of LMS		
25	Leaders clearly know that piecemeal implementation of LMS will only deliver partial results		
26	Leaders preach and practice the A3 framework for strategy deployment		
27	Leaders refer to employees as associates and not as heads, bodies, or masses		
28	Leaders at all levels know and manage collaborative groups for the successful implementation of the lean management system		

3. Value Stream

Number	Points	1–5	Remarks
1	The organization is structured around value streams		
2	Each of the value streams has well-defined ownership		
3	The value streams encompass business units with profit and loss responsibility		
4	The value streams have all the required capabilities to successfully carry out business		
5	Employees at all levels in the value stream have performance appraisal linked to outcomes of the lean management system		
6	Employees show a high level of engagement with the lean management system		
7	Value streams are shaped to serve specific market segments		
8	The company has institutionalized a mechanism to determine the total costs of each of the value streams		
9	The focus of the organization is value stream excellence and not functional excellence		
10	The LMS office regularly makes an assessment of the overall waste in the value stream and shares it with all concerned		
11	Each value stream has a lean maven working for them		
12	Each value stream has its own leadership council to ascertain the progress of lean implementation		

4. Anchors

4a. People

Number	Points	1–5	Remarks
1	Employees clearly know why the company has embarked on a journey of lean management system deployment		
2	Vision and strategic objectives are known to all employees		
3	The entire leadership team, middle management, and bulk of the employees believe that people are the most important asset in the company and they have to be treated with respect		
4	The company places great emphasis on learning and development, and each employee spends at least 10 days on training that improves their effectiveness in their work and his or her ability to work toward the larger vision of the company		

Continued

Continued

Number	Points	1–5	Remarks
5	The company hires employees who are sensitive to customer needs and share the corporate values of the organization		
6	Each employee in the company is evaluated by his or her superiors, peers, customers, and partners		
7	Employees treat every customer interaction as an opportunity to make an impact		
8	Messages conveyed by the workers are given due consideration by management for carrying out ongoing change in the lean management system		
9	Capability-building of employees is looked at as a strategic initiative in the organization		
10	All employees have been trained on problem identification and elementary problem-solving tools		
11	Multi-skilling of employees is taken seriously and reviewed by process owners on a regular basis		
12	The company has a well-defined capability needs analysis process that is reviewed at senior levels		
13	Employees understand that survival in the marketplace requires each one of them to to contribute to making products or services right the first time		
14	Employees are supported, not reprimanded, when they identify problems		
15	Processes and procedures are designed with the participation of employees		
16	There is a great amount of trust between the leaders and employees working on the process, shop floor, or workplace		
17	Employees in a process regularly participate in improvements		
18	Employees look at audits as opportunities to trigger improvement		
19	The organization has a culture of problem prevention		
20	Process associates take the lead to correct problems discovered online		
21	Associates are empowered to take actions that facilitate quick customer recovery		
22	The recruitment process endeavors to ascertain the current behaviors of prospective employees and how they will match up with organizational requirements		
23	Each employee knows his or her customer and the end consumer and exactly what both of them expect		
24	Employees proactively identify the barriers to meeting customer requirements and work toward eliminating them		

Continued

Continued

Number	Points	1–5	Remarks
25	When something goes wrong in a process, employees discover the root cause of the problem		
26	Employees practice value stream thinking, which is about sacrificing their personal and departmental concerns for value stream effectiveness		
27	Employees have a high level of adaptability and quickly metamorphose with changes in customer requirements, technology, and competitive forces		
28	Employees proactively look for wastes in their workplace or business and take the initiative to eliminate them		
29	Employees actively collaborate with members of other functions and departments to solve business problems		
30	When processes change, the employees quickly adapt to new roles and responsibilities with great agility		
31	Regular feedback is solicited to ascertain employee engagement in LMS		

4b. Processes

Number	Attributes	1–5	Remarks
1	For each value stream, there are well-defined end-to-end processes		
2	There is complete alignment on what comprises the value-creating processes		
3	Clear categorization of processes into value-creating, value-enabling, and support processes		
4	Detailed listing and inventory of all processes		
5	All processes have been clearly defined, without leaving them open to interpretation		
6	All processes have a defined purpose and objectives		
7	Processes have defined standards to ascertain ongoing performance		
8	Each process is backed up with procedures that help in their execution		
9	For all processes, the potential risks have been identified		
10	Users in a process clearly know the controls on the potential risks in the process		
11	All end-to-end business processes have clear owners with the authority to design, maintain, and change the processes		
12	All processes and procedures are adhered to as they have been designed and defined		

Continued

Continued

Number	Attributes	1–5	Remarks
13	Processes are managed using well-defined management processes		
14	Process associates deemphasize the identity of their own function, highlighting the identity of the process to which they belong		
15	All key processes have metrics such as quality, delivery, cost, and customer service and business outcomes		
16	There are instances when the organization fails to satisfy the needs of its internal functions but meets the needs of the customers		
17	The sequence and interactions of the processes have been established		
18	The functioning of the organization, business unit, or value stream is not impacted if individuals such as value stream owners or key process stakeholders leave the organization		
19	All processes are linked to policies that govern their functioning		
20	Before processes are changed, the process owners always ascertain the likely impact on other processes		
21	All process associates know the larger objective of the process and their role in making it happen		
22	All processes and procedures are the best known method of doing work		
23	Processes have a number of visual indicators to make deviations obvious		
24	Performance standards of the processes are known by the process associates working on them		
25	All key business outcomes and strategic objectives are clearly linked and managed by processes		
26	Process standardization is looked at as a first step to eliminate wastes from processes		
27	Performance dashboards are displayed so that they are visible to all		
28	All data collection for processes is automated and digitized		
29	There is a hierarchy of dashboards so that people at all levels from CEO to process associate can see the relevant metrics		
30	Takt time serves as a reference for designing all processes		
31	All cycle times in the processes are standardized		

Continued

Continued

Number	Attributes	1–5	Remarks
32	An associate/operator balancing chart is used regularly to see how cycle times compare with takt times		
33	Regular audits of the processes and procedures are carried out to ascertain adherence and reveal wastes		
34	Standard processes are looked at as foundational to continual improvement		
35	Process exceptions are virtually nonexistent		
36	Intervention of technology happens in processes only after they have been leaned and wastes have been removed		

4c. Partners

Number	Attributes	1–5	Remarks
1	Partners are treated as an extended arm of the organization		
2	Trust is what drives the relationship between the company and its partners		
3	The value stream owner gets involved in choosing the partner		
4	The company and the partner are in full alignment on organizational objectives and customer needs		
5	The company believes that partners play a critical role in the success of the organization		
6	The partnership strategy is clearly aligned with overall business and value stream strategy		
7	There are clear service-level agreements between the organization and its partners		
8	Regular feedback is given to the partners on their performance		
9	Regular training programs are conducted for the partner's employees to facilitate improvement in the partner organization		
10	The company does not have a record of unceremoniously dumping partners		
11	The decision on which partner to select is not based on cost but on an assorted set of value-adds that it brings to the company		
12	The organization regularly initiates collaborative projects and joint endeavors to get at root causes of problems		
13	The company works with the partners to reduce partnership cost		

Continued

Continued

Number	Attributes	1–5	Remarks
14	There is a constant endeavor to leverage the strengths and capabilities of both the company and the partners to meet overall organizational needs		
15	The values and attitudes of the partner are important selection criteria		
16	Both parties share their business strategies openly		

4d. Problem Solving

Number	Attributes	1–5	Remarks
1	Problems are looked at as an opportunity in the organization		
2	Problem solving is looked at by all employees as a journey toward getting the best for the company		
3	Each and every member of the organization is exposed to problem-solving tools and techniques		
4	Problems are taken up for solution by all levels of the organization, comprising top management, middle management, junior management, and shop floor associates		
5	The organization has the agility to quickly resolve problems and get at the root causes		
6	The company has a management process to select the right problems to be taken up for resolution		
7	Employees have developed a knack for problem identification, which they have been taught with relevant training		
8	Leaders at all levels are concerned when problems are not identified in a process or workplace		
9	Employees are encouraged and rewarded for identifying problems		
10	The company has an approach for solving problems with the right quality methodology based on the complexity and type of problem statement		
11	The company has a well-defined standard approach to ascertain the effectiveness of solutions implemented		
12	Employees do not jump to solutions, but spend adequate time understanding and defining the problem, followed by a structured approach to resolution		
13	From the CEO to the janitor, every employee is familiar with why–why analysis		
14	For all problems taken up for resolution, the root cause analysis gets at the most fundamental causes		

Continued

Continued

Number	Attributes	1–5	Remarks
15	Each problem has a well-defined action plan comprising what, who, when, and how		
16	The effectiveness of solutions implemented is ascertained regularly by the LMS office and the value stream owner and process owners		

4e. Promotions

Number	Attributes	1–5	Remarks
1	The company has a well-defined communication strategy for institutionalizing lean across the organization		
2	A marketing manager leads the communication and marketing of LMS philosophy		
3	The organization's brand embodies all the elements of operational excellence that it is striving to achieve through the lean management system		
4	The LMS marketing team is successfully persuading the employees in the organization to adopt the lean management system		
5	Multiple channels of communication are being used to promote lean within the company such as meetings, intranets, brown bag sessions, events, brochures, merchandise, and so on		
6	Everyone in the company is a brand ambassador of the lean management system		
7	There is an ongoing measurement to ascertain the effectiveness of communications		
8	Rewards and recognitions are targeted toward all levels of the organization		
9	The reward and recognition program emphasizes team performance while also recognizing individual accomplishments		
10	The rewards and recognitions are designed to drive behaviors that are required for successful LMS implementation		
11	The organization primarily focuses on nonmonetary rewards		
12	The A3 framework and template are used by the entire company for problem solving and continual improvement		

5. Customers

Number	Points	1–5	Remarks
1	The CEO and leadership team believe that the organization needs to differentiate itself on customer service		
2	Employees in the company know who their customers are in the process and also the end consumer that they serve		
3	Retaining existing customers is a key focus area for the leadership team		
4	There is a chief customer officer who represents the interest of the customer in the organization		
5	Customer metrics are an integral part of the overall performance dashboard of the organization		
6	There is an awareness in all process and value stream owners of the impact of changes to processes on the customer		
7	There is a well-defined management process to handle all the queries, feedback, and complaints of the customer		
8	The company has a well-defined voice-of-the-customer strategy to ascertain the changing needs and expectations of the customer		
9	The customer touch-points in all value-creating processes have been identified and customer listening posts have been installed in all of them		
10	The organization has a service innovation cell to create services differentiation in the organization		
11	New processes are designed with the voice of the customer in mind		
12	The organization has institutionalized an empowerment process that employees are supposed to follow when there is a service failure		
13	The concept of customer retention is known to the bulk of the employees of the organization and they demonstrate it in all their actions		
14	The organization identifies specific areas in the customer experience that delight the customers		
15	The leaders pay regular visits to customers to find out their concerns, problems, and headaches		
16	The back-office team members meet with customers regularly to know their concerns, problems, and traumas		
17	The organization has a process to weed out customers who are not profitable to the company		
18	Customers are segmented to facilitate providing unique product and services		

Continued

Continued

Number	Points	1–5	Remarks
19	The company takes customer defection very seriously and installs task forces to find out the causes for defection		
20	The company solicits regular feedback from the employees on its products and services		
21	The company works at creating employee and partner loyalty, as it believes that total customer loyalty is only possible when employees and partners feel loyalty to the company first		
22	Achieving service reliability is a key objective of the leaders of the company		

6. Results

Number	Points	1–5	Remarks
1	The organization has a comprehensive dashboard for sharing performance of financial numbers, customers, employee engagement, processes, partners, and people capability		
2	The dashboard is digitized and captures data on performance at all levels of leadership		
3	There is positive trending of financial results over the last 12 successive quarters		
4	There is positive trending of customer results over the last 12 successive quarters		
5	There is positive trending of employee engagement results over the last 12 successive quarters		
6	There is positive trending of partners results over the last 12 successive quarters		
7	There is positive trending of people capability results over the last 12 successive quarters		
8	The organization is meeting the performance targets for financial numbers over the last 12 quarters		
9	The organization is exceeding the performance targets for financial numbers over the last 12 quarters		
10	The organization is exceeding the performance targets for customer metrics over the last 12 quarters		
11	The organization is exceeding the performance targets for employee engagement over the last 12 quarters		
12	The organization is exceeding the performance targets for partners over the last 12 quarters		
13	The organization is exceeding the performance targets for people capability over the last 12 quarters		

Appendix B

Template for Management Report after LMS Assessment Based on the DEB-LOREX Model

Management Report

Report no.:

Date:

Name of business group:

Name of the CEO or business leader:

Number and list of value streams:

List of value-creating processes covered:

Locations covered:

Names of assessors:

Individuals interviewed:

Findings

1. Opportunities for improvement:

2. Strengths:

Scores:

Specific recommendations:

Signature: _____   Signature: _____
          Lead assessor   Business leader

References

Abe, Mark. "Agile Airline Enterprise," white paper from EDS Global Transportation. California, August, 2005.

Andersen, Bjorn, and Tom Fagerhaug, *Performance Measurement Explained—Designing and Implementing Your State-of-the-Art System*. Milwaukee: ASQ Quality Press, 2002.

Brightman, Igal. "The Trillion Dollar Challenge: Principles of Profitable Convergence." Research by Deloitte Touche Tohmatsu. 2005.

"Cost Efficiency and Revenue in Customer Service." White paper from Right Now Techologies and Peppers & Rogers Group, 2005.

Covey, Stephen R., *The Seven Habits of Highly Effective People*. London: Simon & Schuster, 1992.

Dalkir, Kimiz. *Knowledge Management in Theory and Practice*. Burlington, MA: Butterworth-Heinemann, 2005

Davenport, Thomas, Gilbert Probst, and Heinrich von Pierer. *Knowledge Management Case Book: Siemens Best Practises*, 2nd ed. Berlin: Wiley-VCH, 2002.

Dennis, Pascal. *Getting the Right Things Done: A Leader's Guide to Planning and Execution*. Cambridge: Lean Enterprise Institute, 2006.

Duffy, Jonathan. "The High Price of Low-Cost Airlines." BBC News Online, October 15, 2002.

Feigenbaum, Armand. "Changing Concepts and Management of Quality Worldwide." *Quality Progress* (December 1997): 47.

Frappaolo, Carl. *Knowledge Management,* 2nd ed. New York: John Wiley & Sons, 2006.

Gladwell, Malcolm. *The Tipping Point: How Little Things Can Make a Big Difference*. London: Abacus, 2006.

Gross, John M., and Kenneth R. McInnis. *Kanban Made Simple: Demystifying and Applying Toyota's Legendary Manufacturing Process*. New York: AMACOM, 2003.

Hage, Brian, Matt McKenna, and Herve Wilczynski. "Capturing Hidden Value: Eight Principles for Optimizing Business Processes." www.boozeallen.com, 2006.

Hawks, Karen. "Riding the Wave of RFID." *Navesink Logistics Review* 1, no. 3 (April 2004).

Hedley, Kimberley, John White, et al. "The Paradox of Banking 2015: Achieving More By Doing Less." New York: IBM Institute of Business Value, IBM Global Services, 2005.

Heifetz, Ronald A., and Martin Linsky. *Leadership on the Line: Staying Alive Through the Dangers of Leading*. Boston: Harvard Business School Press, 2002.

Henry, Jim, et al. "Healthcast 2020: Creating a Sustainable Future." New York: Healthcare Institute, Pricewaterhouse Coopers, 2005

Holsapple, Clyde W. *Handbook on Knowledge Management 1: Knowledge Matters,* 1st ed. New York: Springer, 2004.

Horton, William. *Designing Web-Based Training: How to Teach Anyone Anything Anywhere Anytime,* 1st ed. New York: John Wiley & Sons, 2006.

Hoyle, David. *ISO 9000: Quality Systems Handbook,* 3rd ed. United Kingdom: Butterworth Heinemann, 2002.

Hrebiniak, Lawrence G. *Making Strategy Work: Leading Effective Execution and Change.* Singapore: Wharton School Publishing, Pearson Education, 2005.

Hyer, Nancy, and Urban Wemmerlov. *Reorganizing the Factory: Competing Through Cellular Manufacturing.* Portland, OR: Productivity Press, 2002.

Kelling, George L., and James Q. Wilson. "Broken Windows." *The Atlantic Monthly* (1982).

Liker, Jeffrey K. *The Toyota Way,* 1st ed. New York: McGraw-Hill, 2004.

Malykhina, Elena. "Chase to Issue RFID-Enabled Credit Card." *Bank Systems and Technology Magazine* (May 19, 2005).

Marchwinski, Chet, and John Shook. *Lean Lexicon: A Graphical Glossary for Lean Thinkers* Brookline, MA: Lean Enterprises, 2003.

"Mobility Solutions As a Panacea for the BPO Industry." White paper from ValueFirst Messaging Private Ltd. Bangalore/Mumbai, Gurgaon, 2004.

Ohno, Taiichi. *Toyota Production System: Beyond Large-Scale Production.* Portland, OR: Productivity Press, 1988.

Rasmus, Dan, and Bill Crounse. "Future of Information Work: Healthcare 2015." White paper from Microsoft Corp., 2005.

Rother, Mike, John Shook, and Dan Jones. *Learning to See.* Brookline, MA: Lean Enterprises, 2003.

Sarkar, Debashis. *5S for Service Organizations and Offices: A Lean Look at Improvements.* Milwaukee: ASQ Quality Press, 2006.

Sarkar, Debashis. *Lessons in Six Sigma: 72 Must-Know Truths for Managers.* New Delhi/ Thousand Oaks, CA/London: Sage Publications, 2004.

Sharma, Anand, and Patricia E. Moody. *The Perfect Engine: How to Win in the New Demand Economy by Building to Order with Fewer Resources,* 1st ed. New York: The Free Press, 2001.

Smalley, Art. *Creating Level Pull: A Lean Production System Improvement Guide for Production Control, Operations, and Engineering Professionals.* Brookline, MA: The Lean Enterprise Institute, 2004.

Smith, Gerald F. *Quality Problem Solving.* New Delhi: Prentice Hall, 2000.

Suri, Rajan. *Quick Response Manufacturing: A Companywide Approach to Reducing Lead Times,* 1st ed. Portland, OR: Productivity Press, 1998.

Swank, Cynthia K. "The Lean Service Machine." *Harvard Business Review* 81, no.10 (October 2003).

Tiwana, Amrit. *The Knowledge Management Toolkit: Orchestrating IT, Strategy, and Knowledge Platforms,* 2nd ed. New York: Prentice Hall, 2002.

Warwick, Ashford. "Banking via SMS." *ITWeb* (March 10, 2005).

Whalen, Tammy, and David Wright. *The Business Case for Web-Based Training,* 1st ed. Norwood, MA: Artech House, 2000.

Wiegand, Bodo, and Philip Franck. *Lean Administration I.* Aachen, Germany: Lean Managment Institut, 2006.

Womack, James P., and Daniel T. Jones. *Lean Thinking: Banish Waste and Create Wealth in Your Corporation*, 2nd ed. New York: The Free Press, 2003.

Womack, James P., and Daniel T. Jones. *Lean Solutions: How Companies and Customers Can Create Value and Wealth Together,* 1st ed. London: Simon & Schuster, 2005.

WEB SITES

http://sloancf.mit.edu/vpf/popup-if.cfm?in_spseqno=69&co_list=F (MIT School of Management, biography of John Little.)

www.balancedscorecard.com

www.cia.gov/cia/publications/factbook

www.expresshealthcaremgmt.com/200607/analysis01.shtml

www.nist.gov

www.thomasandalex.com/articles/india/why-india.php

Index

A

action, phase of lean breakthrough, 197–200
action plan, 112–13
anchors, 157–94
    installing, 78–80
    reasons for, 80, 157–58
application documents, as sources of waste, 44–45
as-is state, 20–21
    in lean breakthrough, 199
aspirational state, 112
associate balancing chart, 121
A3 template, 191–94
    for problem solving and continual improvement, 191–92
    for strategy deployment, 193–94
audits, 169–70
    of lean breakthrough, 201
aviation industry, relevance of lean to, 4
awareness programs, for capability-building, 85, 90

B

balanced scorecard, 171
banking industry, relevance of lean to, 3–4
batch-and-queue processing, versus continuous flow, 118–20
bias for action, 25
Bisignani, Giovanni, 4

"broken windows" theory, 45–48
brown bag sessions, 190–91
buffer resources, 122–24
build to order, 144–45
build to store, 145
bullwhip effect, 149
business-value-added activities/steps, 16, 115
business-value-added time, 19

C

calculated threshold, 135
capability-building, 83–91
    awareness programs for, 90
    responsibility for, 88
    role of LMS office in, 89
    training programs for, 85, *86–88*
cellular layout, 130–32
certification programs, for capability-building, 85
chief customer officer (CCO), 159–61
chief improvement officer (CIO), key roles, 60
closing, lean breakthrough, 199–200
complexity, in creating waste, 38–39
componentization, 48–49
"consumed" process inputs, versus "used", 98
consumption, lean, six principles of, 42–43
continual improvement
    ongoing, 155
    using A3 template, 191–92
continuous flow, 118–21
corporate dashboard manager, 67